Letters to My Son

To M█████

No matter who we are in life
May you never lose faith in knowing
having love never dies; God
provides for everything

Love you
December 2017

Letters to My Son presents the journey of an extraordinary family dealing with the loss of a son to cancer. One could not help but admire how they listened and acted on guidance that produced a cure to the incurable. And then, the cancer came back. This time it would not be denied. A child's death saddens all parents who hear of it. This book documents a family's passage through grief using letters Mitch wrote to his son, Kelly, after Kelly's passing. The stages of grief a family passes through, and how it returns at anniversaries, big events, and even small circumstances, are poignantly shown.

This is not just a book about grief, however. It's a book about miracles, connections to God, and the heroism required in being human. Kelly's cancer and eventual death presented a choice to his family to either sink into despair or have his life and passing become a gift of love to humanity. It's always a struggle to choose love when pain numbs us, and it was no different for the Carmodys. Fortunately, miracles reinforce our choices as we learn and do. This book is the product of that learning, loving, and doing. That makes it a hero's tale in my estimation. I was really impressed with Meagan's *Soul Talk* on page 116. She's Kelly's sister and was twelve years old at the time, speaking with the wisdom of a sage. One gets the feeling reading the book that whatever "sacred contract," to use Caroline Myss's term, they entered into, they all fulfilled their part in making this a better world.

Letters to My Son is beyond just inspirational. It reminds me of a symphony that balances many noble themes with those of deep despair. It has poems, essays, quotes, photographs, and artwork by Mitch. In the end it has its readers singing a chorus of joy with love that ties us to our maker and each other. This is a book that makes us cry, laugh, feel inspired and rejoice in love. It's a creative masterpiece dedicated to the divine connection in us all. I highly recommend it to anyone.

—Harry McDonald
author of *Touched by Love: A Parable for Today*

Letters to My Son

Turning Loss to Legacy

Expanded Edition

Mitch Carmody

ISBN: 978-1-59298-387-2
Library of Congress Control Number: 2011901994

Printed in the United States of America
First Printing: 2011
Book design by Ryan Scheife, Mayfly Design

15   14   13   12   11   5   4   3   2   1

BEAVER'S POND
PRESS

Beaver's Pond Press, Inc.
7104 Ohms Lane, Suite 101, Edina, MN 55439-2129
(952) 829-8818 • www.BeaversPondPress.com
To order, visit www.BeaversPondBooks.com
or call (800) 901-3480. Reseller discounts available.

For autographed copies, contact the author at www.heartlightstudios.net.

This book is dedicated to my son, Kelly James Carmody, and to all the young children who left the arms of their loving parents too soon.

Neither can they die anymore: for they are equal unto the angels; And are the children of God.

—Luke 21:36

We do not need to proselytize either by our speech or by our writing.

We can only do so really with our lives....

Let our lives be open books for all to study.

—Mahatma Gandhi

Contents

Foreword

A few years ago at a grief conference in Chicago, Illinois, I had the pleasure of meeting Mitch Carmody. Instantly there was a special connection between Kelly's daddy and me. What would develop would become one of the most meaningful relationships of my lifetime. At first glance, Mitch and I might appear to be an odd couple. Our differences have been the fodder for much good ribbing between the two of us. I call Mitch an "old hippy," and he refers to me as "that conservative Baptist boy." Somehow when you put us together, something magical just seems to happen. Mitch has become my teacher, my cheerleader, my confidant, and most of all, my dear friend.

Mitch's wisdom and kindness are unmatched in the arena of those helping the bereaved. Over the years I have watched Mitch develop into one of the most insightful and inspiring presenters on grief and loss. The many losses in Mitch's life, including the death of his beautiful son Kelly in 1987, have given him insight that enables him to examine grief from a unique vantage point.

Mitch's book, *Letters to My Son* has been a heartwarming and healing resource to thousands trying to find hope through their pain. His many articles published in national magazines and on websites are favorites among both professionals and the bereaved.

As an artist Mitch has completed portraits for bereaved parents all over the world. I am fortunate to be among those parents for whom he has created a custom portrait. His portrait of my daughter, Ashley, who died in 2001...is absolutely stunning and one of my greatest treasures (see page 223).

Mitch, through his art, has captured the griever's journey soul of the with his magnificent portraits titled the *The 20 Faces of Grief,* some of which are included as illustrations in this edition. It has been my honor to present workshops using these portraits to help the bereaved connect and reflect, and to help unlock the many emotions that they may be feeling.

As a speaker, Mitch is one of the most in-demand workshop presenters today. His workshops are focused on the concept of "whispers of love," which ask the question: is there life after death on both sides of the equation? Recently Mitch has pioneered a fresh new look at the long accepted *five stages of grief,* which have been used without questions for decades. His S.T.A.I.R.S. theory seems to more accurately depict the different components that the bereaved walk through on our journey and is the basic principle for his model of proactive grieving; it is compelling and fascinating work.

If I were to use one word to describe where Mitch is at today, it would be "peace." Mitch exudes a calmness and serenity in his life despite his many losses. He calls himself an "intentional survivor," and maintains we must somehow turn our loss to legacy.

The bereavement community is blessed that he has chosen to share his art, wisdom, kindness, and insight with us. I am sure you will find this second edition of his popular book, with its updates and recently added artwork by the author himself, as wonderful and healing as the first edition.

Sincerely,
Alan Pedersen, Ashley's daddy
www.everashleymusic.com

Preface

I believe one of the strongest challenges a person can experience in this life is the loss of a child. It is the single most traumatic and devastating reality that I personally have had to bear. There have been years of struggle, but I have found out that, within that struggle, miracles do happen; there is life after death on both sides of the equation. One can survive a significant loss and again find meaning in life, and our lost loved one can help us do that. An important part in healing your grief is expressing your pain and your thoughts to our loved one whom has died and the world at large.

Following the death of my nine-year-old son, Kelly James, on December 1, 1987, I wrote a series of letters to him as a panacea for my grief. He died following a two-year battle with a malignant brain tumor. Every few months I spontaneously penned him a letter when I felt the need to do so. There was no master plan or schedule that I adhered to; I just did it when I did it. For me it was a very valuable tool in processing my grief and moving forward. I know that he received my letters, for he answered me back by fulfilling a request that I had made to him in one specific letter. That response was a miracle all unto itself and will be addressed later in this text.

The purpose of printing these letters and opening my soul and inner thoughts to others stems from a gift that my son has given me: to minister to others and help them to heal and ease the pain in the process of their bereavement. I found out that, when you give, you truly do receive, and in unexpected ways. Helping others has become of prime importance in my life and is a continuing healing process for myself as well. It keeps his legacy alive when I see our lives touch the lives of others.

May the pages of this book give you a tool to use in processing your own grief or helping others to process theirs. I believe that we can communicate with our loved ones who have passed on, and in many various ways they can communicate back to us. I call this phenomenon whispers of love, or the language of soul speak, which is the basis for my workshops held across the country. I have listened to thousands upon thousands of incredible stories that go beyond coincidence. If you are open to the universe, many things can and will present themselves; all you need is an open mind and to have the faith that it can happen.

To better understand the experiences, magic, and miracles referenced in the letters and poems in this text, one should know the history behind them. We were taken on a magical mystery ride that was, and continues to be, life changing. That brief period in our lives has altered us forever. The prologue is an attempt to give you a consolidated version of our life before and after our son's death; I think it will provide the necessary framework to understand many details mentioned in the letters and poems.

—Mitch Carmody

For it is in giving, that we receive.

—Saint Frances of Assisi

It may be the destination that is your goal,

but only on the journey do you discover your soul.

Mitchell H. Carmody

1

Bayport

We were the perfect American family residing in Bayport, Minnesota in the early 1980s. In 1976, I married Barb Wohlers, my high school sweetheart. We soon became expecting parents and moved to this quaint little river town close to the Twin Cities. We bought a grand old gothic house built at the turn of the last century. We settled in comfortably and eventually had two children, a boy and a girl, Kelly and Meagan.

Besides having the typical dog and cat, we had a goat, rabbits, chickens, hamsters, fish, an iguana, and other pets that came and went. I built a huge deck with a wood-fired sauna and hot tub attached. For the kids, I had constructed a unique tree house that was built onto a hollow oak tree. You had to climb into and up through the trunk to access it.

Our house was located on a corner lot, just walking distance from Main Street and the St. Croix River. Summer was a very busy and happy time. Our yard was always filled with kids from the neighborhood. It seemed we could live there forever. We had good jobs; we were healthy, happy, and very content. Life didn't get much better than that.

Then things changed. On March 23, 1984—eleven days after my twin sister Sandy and I celebrated our twenty-ninth birthdays together—she and her two boys were killed in a terrible auto accident. She left behind a very distraught husband and a boy and girl set of thirteen-month-old twins. This event took the whole family by shock; it was a very difficult time for us all. Two years prior to this tragedy, my brother David had died after years of suffering with poor health due to severe retardation from an early age. I had lost my father to heart disease at age fifteen and all my grandparents had died by before I was twenty-five.

With all this death and tragedy in our family, I thought I had a good grip on death and dying. I signed up for hospice volunteer training at a local hospital. They told me I had to wait one year following the death of a close family member. I patiently waited out the year and began my training late in the fall of 1985, completing it in February of 1986. It was then that our world fell apart.

On the last day of my hospice training, a small completion celebration was held. On the way home from that party, I met my wife's car on the road speeding madly in the opposite direction. I flagged her down and she pulled over. My son was resting on the seat next to her, and all she said was, "Dear God, Mitchell, our son is very, very sick. We need to go to the emergency room *now*!" Kelly was seeing double, throwing up and his head really hurt. At the hospital, x-rays confirmed the doctor's fears that Kelly had a brain stem tumor. The tumor was called a *medulloblastoma* and was as big as a baseball; it was malignant, fast growing, and deadly. It had to be removed immediately.

Our lives now concentrated fully on saving our son with any and all means at our disposal. Kelly went through three brain surgeries to treat and remove as much as possible of the malignant mass. We almost lost him twice through the process, and we were very frightened. When Kelly was able to speak again, he told us that he had seen the surgery. He began to recount that he'd watched all the doctors and nurses around his body, and they had been cutting into his head. I questioned him about how he'd seen this and from where in the room. He said that he had "just kinda left his body" and was up in the corner of the room holding hands with Jesus. Although I am very spiritual, I am not what you would call a "Bible thumper." I respect everyone's version of his/ her godhead, admire religious fervor, and believe in miracles. But my beliefs are not limited strictly to Christianity, and Kelly had been exposed to many different cultures. Whatever Kelly saw, it was from no prompting by me.

I asked Kelly what Jesus looked like, and he replied, "He looked like Half-Nelson...ya know, like one of my *Garbage Pail Kid* cards." At that time these collectable cards were very popular with young boys because they were so gross. They were a rather grim parody of the then very popular Cabbage Patch Doll. Kelly adored these revolting cards and collected them voraciously. One of these cards was called Half-Nelson; it was a half boy and half girl depiction. Despite the ignoble nature

Used with permission, ©TOPPS Inc.

of these cartoon caricatures, in the broader spiritual understanding, what Kelly described makes perfect sense. The soul is androgynous— why not Jesus? After all, the ultimate physical incarnation of the perfect spirit encompasses both the anima and animus. Take away our physical human cloak and there is only soul, be it man, woman or child.

Three weeks later, Kelly returned home from the hospital very weak and was partially paralyzed on his right side. His prognosis was not good; he was given only eighteen to twenty-four months of life expectancy *with* treatment. The treatment consisted of a strict regimen of chemotherapy and radiation as well as ongoing physical therapy. During this time he was often sick from the chemotherapy, but he seemed to be growing stronger despite its toxic effects. Our life was comprised of hospital visits as a daily routine and focusing on his recovery.

When Kelly was up to it, we traveled as much as possible; *carpe diem* ("seize the day") became our motto! We took a quick train trip to Chicago one weekend to see the town and its many museums. We traveled to Florida where we saw Disney World and Epcot as well as Disneyland and Universal Studios in California, where Kelly got to ride on E.T.'s bike.

In May, four months following his diagnosis and surgery, Kelly was back in school. It was a difficult challenge for him physically and emotionally. The surgery had left Kelly with serious right-sided weakness. He had a faltering gait and had difficulty writing with his right hand. Undaunted, Kelly learned to write with his left hand and was determined to be a normal child in every way. He did well in school and soon overcame most of his physical challenges. Over the summer Kelly learned how to ride his bike again and even joined the T-ball team. There were ups and downs, bad and good days, but we seemed to be getting back into the mainstream of life. We were confident things would only get better.

To aid us on our journey, we had started a relationship with a very remarkable man by the name of Bernie Siegel. Bernie was a medical doctor but not one of the many attending physicians in Kelly's case at Children's Hospital. Bernie was a surgeon in New Haven Connecticut who had written a book about fighting cancer. We saw a copy at Children's Hospital library; we read it, we liked it, and we embraced the philosophy it contained. The name of the book was *Love, Medicine and Miracles*.

Bernie was a well-respected surgeon who, in 1978, started a cancer–patient support group called ECaP (Exceptional Cancer Patients). While studying the patients he treated, he began to notice the patients who took charge of their disease and were the biggest pain in the rear to deal with were the ones who went into remission more often. They fought to stay alive and questioned everything that was done to them. They wanted to know their disease and fight it with everything at their disposal. Many used holistic approaches that were physically non-threatening, easily done, and only complemented existing medical protocols. This made so much sense, so we took it to heart and began our own regimen to assist in our son's healing.

We started to have Kelly draw some tumor-fighting pictures—for instance, a drawing of *Pacman* eating away at his tumor. We also had him draw a goal picture for the future and one drawing of whatever he wanted just for fun. Eventually, we contacted Bernie in New Haven and began to send him Kelly's drawings so he could analyze them. Bernie would write us back and give us valuable feedback and support. We were so amazed and felt so fortunate that Bernie, a busy surgeon, author, lecturer, and president of the American Holistic Medical Association, would take time to send us handwritten letters and return our phone calls. This man was a remarkable physician for our son, as important as his surgeon and the whole oncology team.

We wanted desperately to save our son, so we did many things. But the most important part, besides our daily prayers, was our belief that what we were doing could make a difference. We explored the power of positive thinking, creative visualizations, guided imagery, the relaxation response, massage, placebos, crystal and light therapy, healing drawings, specialized diets using natural herbs and oils, and many other things. We also explored numerous avenues that did not cause pain and could only help. It bolstered our energies and strengthened our focus. Bottom line—our son seemed to heal faster and experience fewer nasty side effects from the chemotherapy and radiation than he had before. He was feeling better physically, mentally, and spiritually than he had in months; we all were. Summer was in full swing, and we actually started to feel like a normal family again. For the first time in months, we started to believe that we could actually beat this thing.

> *Belief consists in accepting the affirmations of the soul;*
>
> *unbelief, in denying them.*
>
> —Ralph Waldo Emerson

In the fall, the kids started back to school, and despite the difficult challenges, Kelly entered the third grade with the rest of his classmates. We still had to take him out of school for his chemotherapy sessions, and it was at one of these sessions that Kelly told his mother about a questionnaire at school. The children were asked to fill out a form answering questions about themselves, their likes, dislikes, favorite things, etc. One of the questions was: What makes you special? Kelly simply responded, "I'm alive." Together as a family, we focused on this. We appreciated every day that was given us, and our lives were full. The winter of 1987 crept in, and we all hunkered down for the long cold season ahead, thinking only of positive thoughts for the spring.

Following a fairly comfortable long winter's nap, spring soon arrived, and our lives were again propelled into pain and disbelief. In the end of May, just one year after his initial return to school, Kelly went into a full-blown Grand Mal seizure on the playground and was rushed back into Children's Hospital. It was soon discovered that Kelly had a new, fast-growing, large tumor on the frontal lobe of his brain. My son was now given no hope for survival. Palliative radiation treatment was started to slow down the rapid growth of the tumor, but he was given only two months to live. We decided to split up his radiation schedule with two weeks on and then two weeks off.

The Make-A-Wish Foundation granted Kelly a wish, and at his request they agreed to send us to Hawaii for a week. The small, wonderful town of Bayport, where we lived, organized a benefit dance. With the help of our friends, Gina Polk's band Zanth, and local disc jockey Mike Wagner (a.k.a. Donuts), there was a tremendous turnout that raised over $12,000. This enabled us to go to Hawaii for two weeks instead of just one. We saved the rest of the money for the inevitable rainy days ahead.

> Omnia aliena sunt, tempis tantum nostrum est.
>
> Nothing is ours... except time
>
> —a Latin proverb

2

Hawaii and Mexico

The trip to Hawaii was the highlight of our lives. The wonderful people there took us up in their arms and in their hearts. They treated us like royalty. They called Kelly their little brother and catered to his every need. Kelly said he must have lived here a long time ago because he felt like he had come home. His spirit started to soar in Hawaii, away from the doom and gloom of home where well-intentioned visits accompanied with casseroles, flowers, tears and hugs had begun to feel like a premature wake. We needed to get away as a family and recharge our spirits. We did not look back.

We left Hawaii feeling rejuvenated physically and spiritually. Flying back, we stopped in southern California to visit my nephew Jimmy near San Diego. He was living with his biological father, his father's wife, and their three children. His father's wife, Francesca, was of Mexican descent; together they owned a little beach house on the western shore of Mexico's Baja Peninsula. In Minnesota we have cabins up in the north woods; in southern California they have beach houses on the Baja. The house was located in a small (non-tourist) fishing village just south of Ensenada.

In the village near their beach home lived a woman who collected a wild herb called *golondrina* (a type of spurge). With it she made tea that had a purported healing effect that aided in the discomforts associated with cancer treatments. My nephew thought we should meet this lady. We had one more day before we would fly home and begin more palliative radiation. We also needed to refill Kelly's anti-seizure medication. But for now it was carpe diem! We were off to Mexico.

Guided by my nephew's father, Butch, we drove down through Tijuana, past Ensenada, to the peaceful sea village of Maniadera. There we were introduced to Señora Doña Nieves, a genteel older woman well respected in the village. She offered us the tea she had collected and said she would collect more if we needed it. She also mentioned she'd had a vision of this blue-eyed, blond little boy from America that sought a healing from God. She said it was our son Kelly. She invited us to stay overnight and attend her chapel services in the morning. We had flight plans to leave the next morning, but hey, carpe diem rules; flights can be changed; we stayed. Radiation can wait one more day.

We stayed the night at the beach house, and the next morning began the most powerful life-changing experience of our lives.

Doña Nieves (with instructions from God) had built a small chapel behind her modest home. It was to be used for healing and was decorated with pictures of those who had been healed in the past. We were instructed to wear light-colored clothing and to bring fresh flowers for the altar. We were to only have love in our hearts while giving thanks to God for our expected healing.

Before we could enter the door of the chapel, Doña Nieves brushed our heads with fresh herbs and anointed us with strange, pungent oil. We made the sign of the cross and were seated in the room in such a way that we would balance the energies. It all seemed so very ritualistic and strange. We hadn't a clue what was going to happen; all we knew was that it *felt* so right. Kelly also knew, for his face was illuminated with spiritual intrigue. Something powerful was working in this chapel, and we embraced it.

A few other locals and their family members arrived and were seated. Then Doña lit incense and candles while continually splashing holy oil all around and on her body. She seemed to be in continuous prayer and beseechment. Soon two ladies arrived after having traveled a long distance by bus. They seemed to be important to the ceremony, as they were greeted with much fervent prayer and hand waving. One of the ladies, Maria, an older almost toothless woman, was revered as a powerful spiritual healer and was seated in a hardback chair next to the altar. The other lady with her was Marta, who seemed to assist Maria; she sat on a bench located on a sidewall at the front of the church. Once everyone was seated, Doña Nieves began to speak and open the ceremony. Everything was spoken in Spanish, but fortunately my nephew's stepmother was bilingual and interpreted for us.

The service was a strange mixture of Mexican Catholicism coupled with local mysticism. Typical Catholic Mass preliminaries were conducted and then the focus shifted to Maria. The little old woman had gone silent and seemed in deep meditation. She was rocking back and forth in her chair, breathing rhythmically in long, slow, inhalations that whistled through the large gaps in the upper row of her teeth. In a trance like state, Maria slowly rose to her feet, with arms outstretched, and announced in a deep booming voice that our Lord Jesus Christ was here and speaking through this woman. We were asked, one at a time, to come up before our Savior. Maria's persona now seemed to be gone, and Jesus was in the room speaking to us in the first person.

A strange very wonderful energy filled the air as she spoke. You could feel a tangible goodness, a powerful, all-encompassing energy shift taking place in the little chapel. It was as though we were being bathed in some incredible, positive radiation that gave me goose bumps that would not recede. The palms of my hands were continually sweating, and a feeling of undeniable love filled my heart that brought tears to my eyes. Everyone in the room knew something very powerful and miraculous had just happened, something beyond our understanding. God had certainly gotten my attention.

Kelly was called up to stand before Maria. He was a little nervous, but feeling the magic that had entered the room, he nobly walked up to the altar unassisted. Through Maria, Christ placed his hands on Kelly's head while announcing that he was wrapping his purple robe of love around him and that the healing had now begun. He stated that He had placed three lights of healing into Kelly's heart that would be made evident to us within the week. Kelly walked back and whispered to me, "Wow, Dad, I really felt God's hands on my head."

Barb and I were each called individually, blessed, and given our gifts. I was told that I was to be an apostle of God and would be spreading the message of God's love. It was said that I had faith as big as a mountain, and that I was to be the pillar of strength for my family and Kelly's healing. Barb was given the gifts of unconditional faith and was told she was to be an instrument of God's healing powers. Others were called up and given their gifts. Following the last person to receive their gifts, all were called up to stand in front of the altar. Maria then closed her eyes and dipped flowers into holy water and blessed us all. She then gave each one of us a bloom, with instructions to take them home and keep them next to our bed. Kelly was instructed to put his under his pillow for a week.

After this benediction, Maria sat back down and relaxed into her chair. In a few moments her whole body jolted into a severe spasm, lasting only a few seconds. Then she slumped quietly into her chair and was very still. In a moment she seemed to regain her composure and you could tell that Maria was back.

Everyone was given a glass of holy water to drink, and the experience was discussed. There was now an excited and animated energy in the room, and despite the language barrier you could tell something very wonderful and extraordinary had just taken place. Through interpretation, we found out that the ladies were very confident that Kelly's healing would take place, but not without our help. We were told we needed to attend seven more Sunday services for the healing to become complete. They said the Lord would provide the means for our stay to be possible. Marta, the other woman, said we all had lived previous lives and that Kelly's life, this time around, was to bring people closer to God with the miracle of his healing. His healing would be known across the land, forever spreading the message of what faith in God can do. We were told to listen very closely to what Kelly had to say; the hand of God had now touched him.

The ladies closed the service with more hymns that were sung in their local Spanish dialect. Most of the locals joined in, as well as one other little voice: Kelly was singing right in tune with them *in perfect fluent Spanish*. Kelly did not know Spanish, much less a local dialect, and he certainly did not know the ancient hymn. But sing he did! It was a miracle. *Gracias a Dios* ("Thanks be to God").

We were given some of the promised herb golondrina that was to be used to make a healing tea as well as a poultice for Kelly's head. Doña Nieves collected this herb herself, high in the Sierra Mountains. Many years ago, an old Mexican shaman had shared with her the power of this herb and the knowledge of where to collect it. She said it has helped many people in different ways. We were to make a tea for Kelly to drink three times a day, as well as a poultice for his head three times a day. We were also asked to return to the chapel on Friday when some spiritual doctors would be arriving who would want to see Kelly.

We left the chapel that morning awe-struck, trembling and crying tears of joy. The experience left us feeling highly exhilarated yet drained at the same time. Something happened in there that was very real and quite powerful. We knew at that moment, when Kelly sang in Spanish,

God wanted us to stay in this little Mexican village. We also knew we had some very serious decisions to make immediately.

Kelly was still on anti-seizure medication, as well as prednisone, and was scheduled in a few days for more radiation back at Children's Hospital. This was a life-and-death decision to make for our son that could drastically affect the days and months left of his short life. The radiation schedule, which was palliative, would only slow down the rapid growth of the tumor, not cure him. We could hold off on this for a while and see what the next few weeks would bring.

Our biggest concern was taking Kelly off his seizure medication and the prednisone. My wife, who was in the medical field at the time, was very concerned about the medical implications of taking him off his medication in this remote little village so far from a hospital. She decided it would be best to slowly taper what medications we had left until they were gone. The very best (and worst) of modern medicine had failed our son. There was nothing more the medical community could realistically offer him. We were very scared and uncertain, but we put our faith in God and decided to stay at least until Friday so we could meet with the spiritual doctors. This would also afford us the time to discover what *three lights* of healing would be presented to us. We believed that the spirit of God had touched us, and he would continue to guide us on this new journey.

Let me assert my firm belief that

the only thing we have to fear ... is fear itself.

—Franklin Roosevelt

3

Miracles and Magic: The Three Lights

My nephew's father said that we were welcome to stay at their beach house as long as we wanted to (*"Mi casa, su casa,"* or "my house, your house."). With that kind offer, we unpacked our bags and went into the town of Ensenada to shop for supplies and find what God wanted us to find. We felt so connected and knew we would be guided to our three healing lights spoken of in the Sunday service. My wife and I, our gut feelings were together on this, and insights were becoming clearer and seemingly obvious.

While shopping for food, we happened upon a natural health food store to which we were instinctively drawn. Once inside we discovered the store was also a holistic clinic owned and run by a medical doctor turned nutritionist/herbalist. He was also a certified macrobiotic consultant. Nacho, as we learned to call him, was an endearing man with a warm smile and penetrating blue eyes. He also spoke excellent English. We soon found ourselves telling him the whole story of Kelly's illness, from diagnosis to the present moment. He was very excited about the possibility of being able to help Kelly with a macrobiotic diet. He prescribed a disciplined diet of whole grains, brown rice, seaweed, tofu products, and herbs. There were to be no sweets or sugars at all, no fruits or fruit juices, and no dairy products. This was a macrobiotic healing diet to cleanse the body of the deadly residues and toxins from radiation, drugs, and chemotherapy. He also alleged that this diet could reduce existing tumor mass and mitigate further tumor growth.

We all decided to go on the diet and bought bags of macrobiotic vittles, spices, and soy milk. Kelly was not too excited about the prospect of eating all this weird stuff (especially eating seaweed everyday). But it beat going back to the hospital, so he accepted the idea very bravely. This was the first light of healing brought before us, just one day following the service.

I will have to admit I thought the food was disgusting and craved a nice juicy cheeseburger, but it was one for all and all for one. We did it together as a family, and we became quite resourceful with the limited allowable foodstuffs. The food had to be prepared in a specific way, and it soon just became part of our normal activities.

A few days following our initial visit, we returned for more macrobiotic stuff, and Nacho introduced us to Jon, an American acupuncturist who had just started a free (or pay if you can) clinic above Nacho's store. We brought Kelly in to see Jon, who found Kelly's vital energies to be way out of balance and discovered many almost untouchable parts of his body. We had known of these spots under each armpit and the bottom of his feet for quite awhile and had associated them with his overtaxed lymph system. We could not pick him up under his arms without pain; he could not even walk barefoot on the beach. He was still very weak most of the time.

Jon thought that, together with Nacho's diet and visits twice a week for acupuncture, Kelly's vital energies could be restored, which would aid in his recovery. Jon said he had to consult with Sensei, an old Japanese acupuncture master and mentor in San Diego. He did not feel qualified to prescribe the more precise treatments required for this difficult case. Until Jon could speak with Sensei, he began initial treatments immediately on Kelly with the needles. Kelly relaxed and went with the flow, saying, "Heck, dad, these needles ain't nothing. I can't feel a thing!" Thus we found our second light of healing as easily as the first.

For the next few days we relaxed on the beach, enjoying our newfound solitude and experimenting with our macrobiotic diet. On Friday we went again to the chapel to meet with the doctors whom we were told would be coming. Doña Nieves greeted us and, after going through the same preliminary rituals, we were seated this time in the back of the chapel. In the back there was positioned one single cot and a hardback chair; plus a single candle burned, as well as some incense. Fewer people were in attendance than there had been on Sunday, but Doña Nieves, Maria, and Marta were still running the show. As Doña Nieves sprayed the pungent oil about and prayed, Maria seated herself in the hardback chair next to the cot. We were instructed to put our hands in our laps, palms upward, and to close our eyes and pray.

Maria started her loud moaning and strange deep breathing that whistled eerily through her missing teeth. After a few moments, Maria stood up, and in a different voice introduced herself as Emilio Pielroja from the tribe of David. *He* then proclaimed that he was a gifted surgeon who had come to operate on this child in the name of Jesus Christ. Wow… so this was the doctor we came to see! I thought we were going to see some in-the-flesh doctors with spirituality, not doctors *in the spirit*. This seemed very bizarre, to say the least, but everything else had fallen into place thus far. We had to see it the rest of the way through.

This spirit doctor (through Maria) called Kelly up to stand in front of her. Maria then took a bunch of tied herbs and brushed them on Kelly's head and body. Praying all the while, she then brushed the floor in a wide circle around Kelly and then deposited the herbs into an old coffee can of holy water. Grabbing an egg from a bowl full of fresh eggs on the table, Maria made the sign of the cross with it on Kelly's forehead at the tumor site. She then placed this egg in the coffee can with the herbs. More eggs were removed and, one at a time, were rubbed on the back of his head, his chest, and every joint of his body. These eggs were then deposited into the can of holy water as well.

The eggs, we are told, are supposed to pull out the sickness. Maria then stated she would have to perform surgery to remove as much of the tumor as possible. I grab my wife's hand as we gasped together under our breath at this unusual admonition. Kelly seemed very relaxed and compliant with the situation. There was no evidence of scalpels or knives in Maria's hands, so we relaxed (a little) and continued to observe and pray for strength.

Maria recited a prayer and then gave Kelly an injection of anesthetic (in pantomime, of course) into his arm. She then pretended to cut open the top and back of Kelly's head with some invisible tool. She methodically checked around the incision areas with her fingers, diagnosing the situation. With a look of acknowledgment on her face, she proclaimed that, through the power of Christ, this child would be healed. She then grabbed Kelly's young head very compassionately with both gnarled old hands. Placing her ancient lips against his forehead, she began long slow sucking sounds. She increased her fervor and began sucking madly, as if vacuuming out his entire brain. Turning Kelly slowly around, she then repeated this procedure on the back of his head.

Appearing somewhat shaken, Maria stepped back from Kelly for a few moments, regained her composure and asked for the coffee can of holy water with the eggs and herbs. She also requests for a glass of fresh holy water, which Doña Nieves provided for her. Maria took a few small sips of the *fresh* holy water. After swishing it around in her mouth for a few moments, she spit out copious amounts of a white, foamy, yet slimy substance into the can. It reminded me of a melting marshmallow that slowly falls from a stick and into the campfire. She performed this spitting procedure several times, always accompanied with head shaking and a grimace of distaste stamped upon her face.

The can was then set on the vacant front pew. Pointing her finger at the can in dramatic gestures, she cautioned us strongly that the evil, the sickness, was in the can, and that we should stay away from it. "*Que muy malo*!" (very bad) she screamed. Within seconds there were flies swarming all over the can. It was disgusting! The Doña then reprised us once again, saying that the evil was attracting the flies and to stay away. The doctor then announced (through Maria) that we were to come back as many Fridays at it took until he (the doctor) felt the child had recovered fully from this surgery.

While Kelly was still with Maria (and the doctor), my wife, Barb, was called up to assist. Barb was given a small, plastic medicine cup and was instructed to stand close to Kelly. Then Maria, chanting with her eyes still closed, pulled something from the air above her head. She then placed this invisible something into the cup in Barb's hand. Barb was told there were twelve pills placed into the cup, six white and six purple; the white ones were to be taken with water at 6 a.m. every morning, and the purple were to be taken each night at bedtime. Every time a pill was given, we were to say a prayer of thanks for God's healing and profess our love for God. The doctor also stated that he would come at 5 a.m. every morning while we were sleeping. At that time he would dress the wound and change the bandages as well as bless each and every one of us. Maria then sat down on the hardback chair, shook violently a few seconds, then after a slight pause, her small frame slumped quietly and was still.

In a few moments Maria stiffened, stood up, and with a completely different voice and mannerisms, she spoke again. A Doctor Martine had come through her this time. She (he) checked over Kelly quickly and rather brusquely. *He* then said to please follow any given instructions to the letter and everything would be fine. "Next patient please." She then proceeded to take care of the many ailments of the people in the chapel. When she was finally through with the last local seeking help, Maria fell back into her chair looking totally exhausted. Suddenly, she jerked violently and opened her eyes. Then standing up as if waking up from a long restful nap, she smiled and belched loudly in a very nonplused manner. Dousing herself with oil of balsam and acting like she had just arrived, she yawned and said she would see us on Sunday. We hugged her warmly and left feeling dazed and confused.

What the hell had we just gone through? I am a rational man, so I was clueless about what had just happened in there. You could sense, feel, and hear the different personalities that emanated from Maria. It completely blew me away—my senses were reeling. Was this some bizarre cult? Were we being taken in somehow and didn't know it? Whatever it was, it did not matter. Bottom line . . . we all felt so loved. It felt so right, and God help us, it felt so damn good to have hope again.

We were instructed to bring only flowers and our faith with us to the service, nothing more. We offered to pay the bus fare for the long ride Maria and Marta had to take, but we were refused. Nothing was asked of us except to keep our faith strong. Unconditional love costs nothing, and these people wanted nothing more than for us to allow them to do God's work and help heal his children. We had everything to gain. We rejoiced in our great fortune and walked home together hand in hand smiling real smiles for the first time in months. We had found the third light in these spiritual doctors and found that it was good.

> *Faith consists in believing when it is beyond*
> *the power of reason to believe it.*
>
> —Voltaire

In the weeks that followed, we went to more Friday and Sunday services at Doña's chapel. Many wonderful, strange and miraculous things happened at those services, and those who attended were thankful. We received more spiritual medication and advice, which we followed to the letter. My faith was strong, but some nights I would feel like an utter lunatic as I asked my child to pick up these invisible pills in an empty plastic cup. My faith always returned, though, when Kelly would very casually pick the right color pill and swallow it. Not only could he see the pills, he could feel them as he swallowed them. We continued with the acupuncture twice a week and maintained (as hard as it was) a strict macrobiotic diet. We slowly tapered Kelly off his *tangible* medications without incident, seizures, or problems.

In a strange quirk of coincidence, the acupuncturist placed the needles in the very same locations where Maria anointed Kelly with the sign of the cross on the Friday healing services. The acupuncturist also prescribed that we wrap a poultice of whole-wheat flour, taro root powder, fresh gingerroot and water around his head continuously. This was accomplished with a large bandanna he would wear on his head night and day. It was supposed to remove the heat of the tumor and reduce its size. When it dried out we changed it; it seemed to dry out very rapidly.

In time we noticed that it required less frequent changing, as it was no longer drying out so fast.

Accompanying this change, we noticed Kelly was feeling better and had a greater energy level. We could pick him up under his arms, and he would experience no pain. Kelly was out in the ocean on his boogie board and running on the beach *barefoot,* unheard of just a few short weeks prior. Something was definitely happening; our cautious optimism was turning into a real hope for the future. Hallelujah! It was a miracle.

On the sixth Sunday of our stay in Maniadera, we went to the little chapel with Kelly for the last time. We were told our son was healed, his tumor was gone, and that we should go back to Minnesota to our material doctors and show to them what faith in God can do. They declared that our strong faith had healed our son and that his healing would be known all across the land. *Gracias a Dios.*

Actual chapel in Maniadera, Mexico

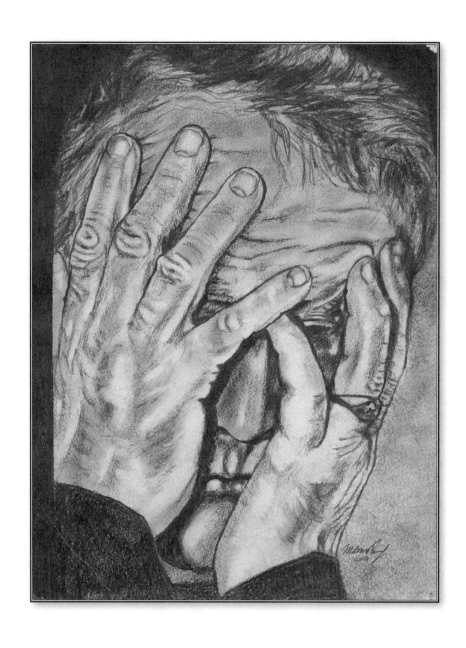

Nothing ever becomes real till it is experienced...even a proverb is no proverb to you till your life has illustrated it

—John Keats

4

The Return

We returned to the United States and made plane reservations to fly home to Minnesota with a miracle in our pocket and hope in our hearts. Our major concern was Kelly's health and the continuation of the methods of treatment we had begun. God had given us a second chance; we wanted to maintain the status quo and promote further healing.

Before flying home and meeting with Kelly's doctors, we found a small house to rent in San Diego. We thought it to best to stay in the San Diego area where Kelly's acupuncturist was located to continue on with his protocol. We would still be near Mexico and be able to travel there for occasional church services to help sustain us in our faith. Our plan was to quickly visit home to meet with Kelly's doctors, and then return to California. We believed that his tumor was gone, but we needed to get the MRI done to substantiate the healing to the world.

The rental home we found was actually in Kensington, a quiet suburb of San Diego. We moved in immediately with only a few sticks of borrowed furniture. We still had a couple of days before our departure, so we had the opportunity to accompany friends to a retreat area nearby in the Madre Grande Sanctuary Park. It was August 17, allegedly a very significant day in the cosmos, when a once in a millennium planetary alignment was to take place. "New agers" called this prophetic day the "harmonic convergence," a day where simultaneously here and in places all around the globe people were gathering together to celebrate the birth of the Age of Aquarius. A new age, one hopefully filled with harmony and understanding, enlightenment, planetary healing, and world peace. What better group of people, what better day, to celebrate the gift of our son's healing, our spiritual epiphany, and our deep gratitude and love for God?

We participated in and experienced some wonderful things that day and evening. There were so many caring, loving people gathered in one place with so much shared belief in the power of love and healing. A large group of us participated in a rebirthing process that was very uplifting and energizing for us all. Afterward, many people stayed behind to lay hands on Kelly and pray for his healing. Fully invigorated, we were now prepared to return home to face family, friends, and the medical community, with the news of our miracle.

Many people thought we had gone off the deep end or that we were somehow being taken advantage of. We were not crazy, and we did not join some peculiar Mexican cult. We definitely had some incredible tales to tell. But crazy? No. The proof of Kelly's miracle was so obvious to us, and it soon would be obvious to the world.

66   *God heals, and the doctor takes the fee.*   99

—Benjamin Franklin

We returned home and immediately were brought down to the mundane realities of our house, our pets, unpaid bills, questioning neighbors, and a very weedy yard. We looked at it all and let it go, for it had no power over us. We were participating in a miracle, and nothing else mattered. Breaking free of the confines of our experiential calluses and cautious optimism, we dared to believe that victory was ours. We believed that God had fulfilled his promise and healed our son. Now we had to get the material proof from our *material* doctors, that our hopes had come true and that we could confirm and substantiate the reality of our miracle. Our next stop was Children's Hospital—and the oncology team.

At Children's Hospital we met with Kelly's primary oncologist to request that an MRI scan be performed. With a raised eyebrow he asked why we wanted this test done when we knew that there was no hope of a remission. We briefly explained the alternative methods of healing that we had experienced and that Kelly's condition had improved dramatically in so many ways. We wanted to know what exactly was happening. He said they would do the test, but cautioned us not to get our hopes up too much. The test was completed, and the results were viewed and examined. It was revealed to us what we knew all along: *there was no sign of the grapefruit-sized tumor that was evident six weeks earlier!* All that was visible was a gray indentation in place of where the tumor had been. The side-by-side MRI scans that were taken months apart spoke for themselves.

The oncologist suggested that possibly the early palliative radiation had done more than was thought possible. He also remarked that, although he did not necessarily believe that our alternative methods of healing had produced these results, he did say, "I guess we all have a lot to learn." After the doctor left the room, the attending nurse jumped up and down with ecstatic joy, hugging and kissing us as we all thanked God together. Words fail to express fully the supreme joy and exaltation that we felt at that moment. We walked down the halls and out the door of that hospital hand in hand, literally kicking our heels up for joy. Victory was ours. Praise God!

Driving home that day from the hospital, we were all giddy with emotion and riding high with the hope and joy that filled our hearts. Soon I noticed that Kelly was looking out the window at all the cars in the rush hour traffic with a very serious, almost sad look on his face. I said, "What's wrong son? Why the long face?"

"Dad, I don't understand why all those people aren't looking over here at us. Don't they know a miracle has just happened?"

To me every hour of the light and dark is a miracle.

Every cubic inch of space is a miracle.

—Walt Whitman

Dare to dream.

5

A Journey in Faith

"Where do we go from here?" That was the biggest question in our minds and hearts. We had been touched by the hand of God and experienced a miracle first hand. An experience such as this can change your life and that of countless many other lives forever. A miracle is analogous to the act of dropping a small stone into a calm pond. It sends out ripples in all directions, touching hearts and changing lives *ad infinitum.* The miracle is a gift; it is faith, which activates that part of us that receives internal divine guidance. Call it vivid dreams, visions, voices, a psychic connection, spirit guides, or guardian angels—it all boils down to relying on that good old "gut feeling."

We had gone that far relying on our gut feelings and had made some extremely important, life-changing decisions very quickly. We had dropped off the edge of the earth for six weeks and had come back with a miracle. Some friends and family thought we might have needed deprogramming, or that we were being ripped off in some way. Others had no idea what had happened to us. We had a lot of phone calls to make.

Word spread rapidly of our return and the miracle of Kelly's healing. It hit the local newspapers and radio waves. Soon we were inundated with calls. We relayed the story with great enthusiasm and spiritual fervor. It was like we were plugged into some powerful God energy that could not be dissipated. Nothing was an obstacle, nor was any problem too large or person too small. Nothing could stop the momentum of our miracle in action. We had to continue with the plan that God had prepared before us. Kelly's tumor was gone, but our journey had only just begun.

Barb and I arranged for a further leave of absence from our employers, which was readily granted. Barb and Kelly flew back to the little rented bungalow in San Diego to continue on with Kelly's treatments. Our daughter Meagan and I stayed behind in Minnesota for two more weeks. In those two weeks, I put the house on the market, sold most of what we owned, and arranged for the placement of pets and plants. I rented a fourteen-foot U-Haul truck and packed it up with the bare necessities of life. I hitched up my wife's car to the back of the truck, and we said our good-byes. Meg and I were off to join our family in San Diego.

In San Diego we put the kids in school, found jobs, and prepared to make a new life. It was not easy, but we made it work and continued with Kelly's alternative treatments. This new period of relatively calm times was short-lived, however, for within a month Kelly was getting sick again. At the hospital, it was confirmed that the cancer was back, and that it was spreading rapidly throughout the brain and down the spine. It was *post-haste* back to Minnesota to be with friends and family. Kelly was dying.

The dark clouds were back. It felt as if though we had been kicked in the gut. We had so much hope and had worked so hard. We had done everything humanly possible to save our son—there was nothing more that we could do. It was so unfair. We were angry at God, angry at ourselves, angry at the acupuncturist, angry with the little Mexican church, angry with the doctors who could do no more and just damn angry at the world. It is probably this anger that gave us the needed energy to move halfway across the country one more time. Kelly and Meagan needed us more than ever, and we needed to be home.

Barb made arrangements to fly back to Minnesota with both kids and stay with her mom and dad. I stayed in San Diego to pack up, settle affairs and await the moving van that my wonderful mother-in-law had graciously arranged and paid for. Once back home, we rented a town-house by the month. It was a place to set up hospice care, a place for Kelly to die. We traveled a little and celebrated Kelly's ninth birthday with all his friends and family. We had an emotionally difficult Thanks-giving, as it is hard to be thankful when your child is dying. We were preparing for that fact. No more attempts were made for a cure. Our efforts were comfort measures to let Kelly live his life to the fullest that his abilities would allow.

By the end of November, Kelly was very weak and sleeping later in the mornings. A Minnesota winter was in full swing, with its snow, ice and cold north winds. December was just around the corner, and I was afraid Kelly would not see another Christmas. Most of our days were consumed with short walks, hot baths, and watching movies. On the last Sunday in November, after a typical leisurely morning, we took the kids to see the movie, *Planes, Trains and Automobiles.* John Candy was one of Kelly's favorite actors, and he was anxious to see the movie. We were all laughing very hard during the film (a very welcome catharsis). But we soon noticed Kelly was getting quiet and fidgety; he wanted to go home.

We left the theater and stopped by a video store to pick up some movies. We gave Kelly some of his liquid morphine (which we had been using with greater frequency), gave him a hot bath, and set him up on the couch to watch some movies. The tumors in the spine made it difficult for Kelly to sit in a chair for a long period of time. Lying on the couch with lots of pillows and blankets was where he seemed most content and relaxed. In a few hours Kelly announced that he just wanted to go to bed for the night. It was only 4:30 in the afternoon, but Kelly knew what he needed. Together we crawled into my bed for a late afternoon nap.

Curled up in our warm waterbed, with daylight fading into darkness, I started to drift off to sleep while staring at my son's beautiful face. Seemingly aware of my gaze, Kelly slowly opened his eyes, reached over and very weakly brushed the back of his hand against my stubble of a beard and said, "Dad...I love you." With that said, he rolled over and went immediately to sleep. I told him I loved him as well, tucked in his covers, and kissed him on the head goodnight. Realizing that there were tears pouring down my face, I got up out of bed; something was happening. Kelly knew it, and I felt it.

At 7:30 in the evening, Kelly came stumbling out of our bedroom looking dazed and confused. He said, "What happened? Where's mom?" I told him that after we had gone to bed for our little nap, Mom had gone shopping. Kelly replied that he had not remembered coming home from the movie or even going to bed, and he was confused that it was so dark outside. Clearly perplexed, Kelly looked at me very seriously and said in an exasperated tone, "Dad, I need to clear my head. Let's go for a frigging walk!" I hugged him tightly and said, "Sure son, I need to clear my head too." We dressed warmly and went for a short walk. Kelly was tired most of the time now and was becoming incontinent, and he was requiring stronger doses of morphine more consistently. I knew that his last days were approaching quickly, and as far as I was concerned, he could do or *say* anything he wanted to.

The next day we called our neighbor Bonnie, a friend and certified hospice nurse, to come and see Kelly. We told her of his recent changes and that we would appreciate her opinion on his condition. We were now preparing for his death. It was becoming real, and we needed assurance that it was. Bonnie spent several hours with us and observed Kelly very closely. She told us that Kelly was indeed exhibiting classic symptoms that precede an imminent death. She felt that Kelly had only days left, possibly a week or two, but it was evident he was slowly slipping away. He could easily slip into a coma or die at anytime. We had no plans for dramatic, life-saving measures—only pain relief, comfort, and lots of love.

After Bonnie left, I went shopping for a three-week supply of groceries, and other necessary comfort items that we might need. Kelly slept for most of the day. My wife Barb made all the necessary phone calls to family and friends to inform them that, indeed, Kelly was dying. "Come visit very soon," she said.

Later that evening two of Kelly's best friends, Jason and Dustin, came over to say goodbye to Kelly. Kelly was very weak and was unable to communicate with them, but he was fully aware of their presence. Although he did not talk with the boys, he did raise his hand slightly and weakly waved goodbye as they departed. His left eye was now staying open all the time and needed constant wiping and lubricating. Kelly was no longer interested in food, and even drinking water had become difficult. We only moved Kelly from couch to bed or to the bathtub as needed. As weak as he was, he did not want to be carried, and we would walk him like a marionette. Evening soon turned to night, and we *all* slept with one eye open, unsure what tomorrow would bring.

The next day was December 1, and Kelly was, for the most part, unresponsive on the couch. His lips and nails were turning blue, and he was still and very pale. Bonnie (the hospice nurse) came over, as well as many close friends and family, knowing this would probably be his last day with us.

Our daughter Meagan was only five years old at the time and needed a break. But she did not want to be gone too long from her "brover," and we wanted her there should Kelly pass on. We sent her off with the Scheels, good friends from Bayport, who took her out for pizza and an escape from the death vigil. They would call us with a number where they could be reached, should his condition worsen.

While Meagan was gone, Kelly's breathing became very erratic and shallow, Bonnie said, "It's time. You better get a hold of Meagan quickly." The Scheels had called previously with a number at the pizza place where they had gone, and we frantically called it, talked to them, and said, "Please hurry." Kelly's breathing was now very shallow and the "death rattle" evident. Time was of the essence; we were not certain Meagan would make it home in time. Kelly had now been totally unresponsive for hours, and with his breathing rate we knew it would only be minutes. Barb and I were kneeling next to Kelly, holding his hands, praying Meg would be there soon. Suddenly we heard a knock at the door, followed by Meg's cheery voice, "I'm home, Kelly."

At that moment Kelly opened his eyes, moving them toward the sound from the door. When Meagan reached the three of us on the couch, she grabbed Kelly's hand and said, "Bye bye Kelly, I love you. Sorry I'm late."

He looked at her and sighed one last breath. You could feel that his spirit was leaving his body. His whole face, previously paralyzed on one side, now relaxed. His eyelids opened slowly, revealing those beautiful, cornflower-blue eyes that glowed bright and clear with a look of serenity and peace. I could even see a twinkle in those eyes, as if he had just discovered some great secret. When his face relaxed, Kelly's smile also returned. It was a smile we had not seen in almost two years. Looking out at no one (that *we* could see), the light in his eyes faded and his lids slowly closed. The spark gone—forever.

Now that Kelly had died, we had to make arrangements for the body, as well as calling the local sheriff to report his death. We also made many phone calls to friends and family who were not present at the time of his death. With Kelly still lying on the couch in the same position that he had died, many friends and family showed up to give their last respects and support us in our time of need. In that tiny townhouse, together with close friends and family, we laughed, cried, looked at photo albums, and shared many stories well into the evening.

Our minister arrived late, and he was surprised to see that Kelly's body was still lying on the couch. We had many candles lit and were playing Christmas music as he walked in. He later commented that it seemed more like a Christmas gathering then the scene of a recent death. He said it was awe-inspiring, a celebration of life that brought tears of joy to his eyes and not those of pain. There were angels in the room with us that night, and who so ever entered that room *felt* it.

It was not until much later that the sheriff and the coroner showed up to witness the death and remove the body. I picked up my son's body to carry him down to the awaiting hearse when my brother-in-law Paul stopped me before I descended the stairs. He said, "Mitch, as Kelly's godfather, I held him as he was baptized. Can I please hold him once more?" There at the top of the stairs, I passed my son over to Paul once again, as I had done nine years earlier—only this time Paul kissed him goodbye.

We had already begun funeral plans while Kelly was alive. We made it a celebration of life and the miracle that was Kelly. The church was filled with hundreds of people, many of whom were children. Numerous endearing stories were shared, and joyful songs were sung. We had no graveside interment; Kelly's ashes were sent to Hawaii where friends released them from an airplane into the live volcano Mauna Loa. In lieu of a stone marker, we purchased a wall plaque at Children's Hospital with his signature and the words, "Let your heart-light shine."

You are the light of the world. A city set on a hill cannot be hidden.
Men do not light a lamp and put it under a bushel basket. They set
it on a stand where it gives light to all in the house. In the same way,
your light must shine before men so that they may see goodness in
your acts and give praise to your heavenly Father.

—Matthew, 5:14–16

Kelly experienced a healing in Mexico, but unfortunately, it was not
a cure. I learned through the whole experience that there is a big difference between a healing and a cure. Sometimes they may happen
together, but usually I believe they are separate things—one spiritual,
the other physical. We experienced both, but it was the spiritual healing
that has endured and enriched our lives, and has hopefully made this
world a little better place.

The physical aspect of healing (i.e. a cure) is, at its best, intrinsically
limited, for life by nature is terminal. We accept both the physical death
and the spiritual healing. The first is to be able to move on with our
lives. The latter is to be able to more fully embrace our own spirituality. We must grow from our experiences to help nurture ourselves, our
family and help to heal the human condition in general. Look for the
gift encapsulated in your grief and find the golden opportunity that is
presented to you. Share your life and you will find that, through helping
others in their pain, you will alleviate yours, for it is when you give that
you truly do receive.

You must give some time to your fellow men. Even if it's a little thing,

do something for others—something for which you get no pay

but the privilege of doing it.

—Albert Schweitzer

To Mom, Dad, and Meg

From Kelly
—song lyrics by Laurie Pelnar

I didn't mean to make you cry
But you know I had to say goodbye
I loved you so and I know you know

I'll stay real close beside you
I'll be the light, the light that guides you

Look for the star the brightest one
That one that shines beyond the sun
I'll shine for you and see you through
With loving warmth and laughter

The tears will pass into a song
A song to echo your whole life long
Know I love you and I'll always be
The light that guides your fantasies

When you think of me please let it be

With rainbows and with laughter

The hurt will pass the love will last

Look for light, the light that guides you

You gave me everything I could wish

Your smiles your laughter and your kiss

You made my life a fantasy; my last days were ecstasy now

I'll be the light, the light that guides you.

Suffering will come; trouble will come—

that's a part of life—a sign that you are alive.

—Mother Teresa, (May 1975)

The Letters to Kelly

The seven letters I had written to Kelly are printed here in their entirety as they were written and are not edited. I did not want to lose any of the emotion that was present at the time of the writing. Following each of the letters is a brief postscript from today's perspective. Not only is this a reflection of that period of time when the letters were written but also it provides details that support statements or settings mentioned in the discourses with my son.

Following each postscript are several poems that I had written at or around the time that each of the letters were written. The poems were written for others that were experiencing grief in their lives or simply for the solace of my own soul. Regardless of their inspiration, they vividly portray the emotions that I was feeling at that time. They also tend to illustrate the combination of the many elements of grief: shock, denial, anger, hope, isolation, bargaining, depression, and acceptance, to name a few. They are not really stages but components of the grief journey that you can and will experience as you process your loss. No one grieves the same way or on the same schedule. It is a roller coaster of emotions that come as they may. You grieve as *you* grieve, and it takes as long as it takes.

For a Dying Child

by Nancy Lee Carmody, (Kelly's aunt)

If fish could only half swim

or birds half fly

like an agreement to be half in love,

then maybe a child could half die-

with an agreement to be back in time.

How much easier the parting could be

knowing the promise of return.

But fish swim full hilt

and birds hit the air without remorse

most lovers would jump over the moon

to be overheels in love.

So a child dies and all we can do

is believe in his soul.

If we believe in this

and the new life that is his,

we may have more in common with him

than with the living.

FIRST LETTER

February 20, 1988

Why am I so special?

I'm special because I'M ALIVE.

—Kelly Carmody (1987)

2-20-88
Dear Kelly,

It has been almost three months since you have left us and I miss you terribly at times. I replay your last few days over and over. I feel that I should or could have done more. I knew your time was very close, but then again I didn't really know how close. It was hard to see you degenerate so quickly, feeling impotent to change the devastating progression moving through your body. You were barely speaking and I sometimes wondered if you knew what was going on. I know you did not want to talk about death and I understand why. You wanted to live each moment without the realization of the shadow of death that was so obviously imminent. When you did make your transition, you looked so happy and at peace.

It took a lot of guts and strength with pure love to wait for your sister Meagan to come home before you left. You really did love her a lot, didn't you? I know she misses you a lot, although she is enjoying the attention she gets now that you are not the center of our universe.

Your funeral, as I am sure you saw, was breathtaking! It touched all that were present and will for years to come. You gathered quite a faithful following, my son, and have changed many lives in your short term here. You must be resting for quite awhile after such a long arduous battle. I am looking forward to a visit from you sooooooo much! I don't want to try too hard, but I am always ready when you are up to it ol buddy.

I remember our short little walks around the snow and ice of that awful townhouse. Those walks were precious to me son, and it does hurt to think about it. I remember with joy our trip to North Carolina. I know now it was something you had to do before you left. I am so glad we did it and you did so well out there.

We had a kind of non-existent Christmas without you there pal. It seems like I slept through it with vague dream memories. I am sure your Christmas was much better, probably more of a birthday party. Which reminds me how glad I was to have had your birthday party; I still watch the videos of it and ache.

I loved your message of your signature left in the pew at church and the "I'm Alive" song on the radio after the funeral you arranged for us to hear. Very subtle! Now get back with the code word to somebody, you turkey.

I hope you were happy with the shadow box I made for Mom from you. I felt guided by you to do it. It was symbolizing your moment of separation from the body as your spirit flew up the rainbow to unite with God. I wanted to keep your healing stone in a safe place, so I placed it inside. Your Mom is doing much better; you must be helping her now that you have rested a bit. Visit her soon son and wrap your arms around her and let her gaze into your beautiful blue eyes; then get to Meg and finally to me, Bubba.

How do you like our new house? Isn't it beautiful with the pond and everything? You would have loved it here, I know. We are doing the best we can to rebuild our lives without you and try to find happiness and joy again. I love your mother and sister very much and will do anything to make them happy. I think this new house is a good idea and we shall heal faster with it.

I am glad that you can now play with your dog, Maple again, as he has joined you recently. Have you seen Grandpa and Grandma Carmody, as well as Grandpa and Grandma Great? I bet you have seen Aunt Sandy with Jason and Travis already. I am feeling pretty good now Kelly and it is no reflection on my love for you. I just know you are where it really is at and we have to come home to you. But until that day, please pay us a visit. I MISS YOU SO MUCH!

If you can arrange for a sign from you this spring, like something growing from our yard, that would be neat and I WILL notice. I will write again later sometime. Know that I love you and still need your love.

—Dad

———————————————

This letter was the first one that I had written posthumously to my son. It was penned some three months following his death. It reflects the post-shock period that soon follows the wake/funeral and the subsequent intense grieving period. During the eighteen months that we battled with his cancer, from its onset to his death, we had totally focused our lives on his recovery. Now our lives were focused on accepting his loss and working on our own recovery.

The funeral service at the church was packed with people, with many children sitting in front of the altar. In the back there was standing room only. We had the church filled with purple helium balloons that were then taken outside the church following the service and released into the cold December sky. Across the country friends and relatives released balloons at the same time. As we were leaving the church, my niece came running over to me and said, "Look what I found." She had been rummaging through the envelopes on the backrest of the pew and found one that had been written on. It was Kelly's signature! The last time he had been in that church had been seven months earlier.

When we lived at the Mexican beach house, Kelly had discovered an old Neil Diamond album. At the time, Kelly had been into heavy metal and rap music but seemed drawn to this album. On the album there was one song that Kelly really liked called "Ensenada," which was where we were staying. The album also had a song that Kelly loved and played over and over again; it was called "I'm Alive." The verses were so appropriate and reflected Kelly's positive attitude in Mexico. I had never heard of this song before and have only heard it on the radio once since those days in Mexico.

After the funeral was over and we went to some close friends' house for refreshments, I heard it again. We had been at the house several hours, and I went out to warm up the car (December in Minnesota). Once it was running, the radio started playing *I'm Alive* right at the beginning of the song. I ran quickly inside and got my wife and friends; together we listened to that song in the cold winter evening and cried—tears of pain, mixed with tears of joy—for we knew Kelly was saying that he was *truly* alive. This was the beginning of some very important spiritual affirmations that lifted our hearts for those first few months after his death.

Following this intense period of eighteen months, there was a tremendous feeling of relief. Together, with the love and energy from family and friends, we felt buoyed up despite our pain. We bought a new house—a nice suburban rambler on the edge of a park. My wife and I returned to our old jobs; our daughter Meagan returned to school and made new friends. After three months, the condolence cards had stopped arriving, and most people thought we were getting on with our lives, that things were getting better. Very few people know the true depth of pain and how long it can last.

What shall we do with this strange summer, meant for you—

Dear, if we see the winter through

What shall be done with spring?

—Charlotte Mew

HELLO AND NOT GOODBYE

My son, you have seen the worst of times
but yet have seen the best
life may have seemed unfair to you
up to this your final rest.

We did everything that we could do
to remove the evil curse
the disease that caused such misery
and eventually got worse.

This evil thing has taken your life
and violated your chance to live
cut short your youth's vitality
with all it had to give.

It may seem hard to understand
that good can come from bad
that happiness and joy can come
from times so very sad.

But good things have already happened
as now you can clearly see
your vision of a higher power
that sets our spirits free.

You have given the Lord to us
in ways no one ever could
made our eyes to see his light
our hearts to feel his good.

We have seen his miracles
made possible through you
although your life was very short
you brought us hope . . . that grew.

A stronger faith in our Lord
a deeper love in our hearts
a different way of looking at life
in all its intricate parts.

So my son, your life was not wasted
but shared with all mankind
and everyone, if we look
will find the tie that binds.

The tie that binds all human hearts
to each and one another
and when death does come our way
it's shared by each sister and brother.

So today we are sharing you
a celebration of your life so brief
the saying of our unsaid goodbyes
and the beginning of our grief.

Grieve we must for our tragic loss
for your eyes so heavenly blue
sorrow for the empty void
that was once filled by you.

Our grieving will not be easy
in fact it will be long endured
we all loved you so very much
and had hoped you would be cured.

But you have ascended to the Father
a fact we must accept
and for all you have given us
we are forever in your debt.

Good-bye my son, you're in good hands
though I will miss you in my own
but I will see you always
from the seeds that you have sown.

Thanks for having been my son
I'm proud to be your dad
and until our souls again unite
I'll remember all we had.

Now as you soar on eagle's wings
over rainbows in the sky
whisper to me upon the breeze
hello and not good-bye

It is never any good dwelling on goodbyes.
It is not the being together that it prolongs
—it is the parting.

—Elizabeth Asquith Bibesco

For Barbara on February 14, 1988

My darling I am not sure what to say
nor even what to do
to make this very special day
unique and true to you.

We have gone through so many things
from last year at this time
traveled our country over
from frigid to tropical clime.

Experiencing great joy and loss
alternating and together
clinging desperately to our faith
bound to a cancerous tether.

No one can truly be ready
to do what we had to do
be prepared to battle
and yet to each other remain so true.

True to our own identity
and true to us as a whole
putting all our strength together
to fight a common goal.

Cancer had declared war on us
we dared to fight back
examining life's priorities
and picking up the slack.

A battle plan was made
our enemy defined
we geared up with ammunition
a declaration of war was signed.

Sacrifices had to be made
we were motivated to win
no obstacles were ever too large
no ice ever to thin.

We forged weapons of pure energy
that were smelted in our hearts
with guidance from our God
and the knowledge that He imparts.

He informed us where to go
told us what to do
with us every step of the way
in places old and new.

We had many victories
but also suffered loss
their outcomes as flippant
as a coin in mid-air toss.

Though many battles were won
we lost the two-year war
as cancer beat the victim
and claimed the final score.

The scars of war are very deep
and take time to heal
as any survivor of any war
can tell you how we feel.

Everything has to be rebuilt
future plans made anew
many things to overcome
before our healing is through.

Post-war years can be very hard
with flashbacks of hurt and pain
the causalities find a better life
it's hard work for those who remain.

But hard work we are used to
as together we can fight
the hassles of the present
to make the future bright.

We have always had each other
though differences there may be
communications can break down
setting trouble free.

I know that we can handle it
our love is very strong
our souls are bonded together
to last a lifetime long.

That lifetime is here and now
I have never loved you more
and someday as a family
on eagle's wings we'll soar.

Until that glorious day
when we reunite with our son
we'll live each day the best we can
praising God when the day is done.

SECOND LETTER
April 2, 1988

And when life's sweet fable ends,

Soul and body part like friends;

No quarrels, murmurs, no delay;

A kiss, a sigh, and so away.

—Richard Crashaw
(*Temperance,* 1652)

4-2-88

Dear Kelly,

What can I say except that I miss you terribly!!! The past week my thoughts have been on you every minute of the day it seems. I watch TV and see ads for a new horror film and I think of you, I see ads for a new monster toy and I think of you. We went on a hayride last week and I thought of how much you would have enjoyed that.

Tomorrow is Easter Sunday and we are reminded of the resurrection of our Lord. It is hard for me to feel anything except sadness. I see other fathers with their sons and it cuts through me like a knife. I know eventually things will hurt less and I know you are in the best of all places, but I cannot help feeling lost and helpless.

It seems I am covered by a thin invisible film of despair that cannot be shed or penetrated from within or from without. I do not know if this film will last a lifetime and I will learn to live with it or it will eventually dissipate.

I love our new home, your mother and Meagan dearly, but the desire to be with you is very strong. I would never dream of exiting this life on my own accord, but I could easily leave without remorse. These are my feelings now and it does not take away my love and devotion for your mother and sister. The reality is we are and will be here until our missions are through. I know I will find joy again but never quite the same intensity of joy.

I still am longing for a visit from you and I will do more on my part to try and communicate. Please find the strength to come to me. Sometimes I feel we kind of pushed you out the door, wanting the "unknowingness" to be over with. I admit in certain ways I did want it to be over, not knowing what else to do, but more than that was seeing you waste away to a shell like my brother David was something I could not bear to see. I hope you have had a long rest and will help me find my way! Be with me at the Indian sweat lodge next Friday if it can be arranged.

I love you forever.

—Dad

This letter to Kelly was written five months following his death and illustrates the end of the "up" period that the first letter reflected. Nobody, except for some very special friends, ever brought up Kelly's name, and we were expected to slide right back into the groove of normal life. The relief we now felt turned into a cavernous void that seemed impossible to fill. We had done so much for so long that, initially, the void was a period of physical, mental, and emotional rest that gave us the illusion of doing okay. Soon the void turned from rest to restless. We were used to doing so much and being so focused that we then felt lost and without purpose. I started feeling guilty for not having done more and especially guilty for the nights that I would check on him, praying that God would take him, to end the madness and the pain.

The Godsend that helped out during this time was the Indian sweat lodge that I referenced to in the second letter. I had heard of the Native American sweats held on Prairie Island and that the tribal chief at that time was Amos Owen, who had a vision to bring the healing power of the sweat lodge to non-Indians. I definitely needed a healing but, more importantly, I was worried about my wife. She was not doing well at all. I could attend the sweat ceremony, but she could not because she was in her phase of the moon (menses), which prohibited her from participating. I fasted for a three-day period and then went to the sweat lodge alone. That particular evening there were a lot of people in attendance, which required that they hold two ceremonies in order to accommodate everyone who had traveled there.

Being a new initiate, I had to wait for the second ceremony, which did not start until after ten p.m. My wife had expected me back by that time, so, tired of waiting up for me, she had gone to bed. When I was in the sweat lodge, time lost all meaning, with the drums, the chanting and the intense heat, it became a different world. Amos said that this special ceremony was for the healing of all the relations, and we passed the pipe of burning Kinnikinic and beseeched the ancient grandfathers to come to the lodge and take our healing requests. An incredible feeling of peace and power filled the small enclosure. Healing requests were made, and tears were shed freely that commingled easily with the rivers of pervasive sweat. I requested that the grandfathers go to my wife and give her a healing, one that she so desperately needed. When the sweat lodge ceremony was over, I sat by the fire awhile, lost in the reverie of one of the most powerful spiritual experiences of my life.

I arrived home well after midnight, and I was surprised to find my wife still up. Her face was radiant, and she was smiling and crying at the same time. "Tell me about your sweat ceremony, Honey, but first let me tell you of the most incredible experience I had tonight." She said she had retired early, at about ten p.m., figuring the sweat was running behind. Later on, she awoke with a start at about eleven p.m. to hearing Kelly calling her name. She got up and walked out on to the upper patio deck, and there she felt the presence of Kelly surround her. He said that he loved her and was happy, and she could feel him hugging her and could actually smell his wonderful smell. Barbara looked so beautifully radiant and happy as she relayed this, that I knew it to be true. She had this experience at the same time as I had beseeched the grandfathers to go to her aid.

In this letter I had asked Kelly to be at the sweat lodge with me. I know with the help of the grandfathers that he was there and they had guided him to his mother when she needed him most. God works in mysterious ways, as we had been finding out. There are miracles out there just for the asking. All you need is faith.

These incidents helped immeasurably in the healing process, but it still takes a long time. There is no way around grief, only through it, and it takes as long as it takes. The poem *Empty Fullness* that immediately follows this postscript was written the day after I wrote the second letter to Kelly and truly depicts what my feelings were at the time.

EMPTY FULLNESS

What is this grip that holds captive my soul;
Clenching my heart so hard to console?
Where is life going, what does it mean?
The mystery of life is yet to be seen.

Did I not have lofty ideals and dreams?
Carefully plotted plans die also it seems.
The future seems non-existent; each hour is now;
the past, a flood of pain, that I endorse and allow.

The pain is reality and breaks the omnipresent spell
with it comes a clarity ... a crack in the shell
It lets the real world in for only a moment or two
and in that instant, I know I'll get through.

The pain rings clear of the awful truth of perdition
not a statistic or concept but the reality of condition
A glimpse in the darkness that the loss is for real
and gut-wrenching agony is all that I feel.

The aching diminishes as non-reality returns,
every day life carries on, while my sorrow still burns.
I have traveled this path many times before
and recognize the signs that can open the door.

I cannot seem to find the panacea for my grief,
what had worked before, now gives no relief.
I seem destined to be caught in this web of non-being,
that feeling of empty fullness … perception without seeing

This space in time seems not to progress,
every day seems like a dream that was dreamt in duress.
This feeling of futility I hope will transcend;
I have so much to learn and more to comprehend.

There is so much I want to do and my love I want to share,
I need again to smell the flowers and heal my dark despair.
Someday the light will come and illuminate my way
shadows will fade and so will the gray.

The sun will rise with beauty; I will again feel its embrace;
the rain will feel good once more as it falls upon my face.
The wind will blow sweet fragrances that I can smell anew
rainbows will again be enchanting in all their glorious hue.

Tomorrow will again have meaning; the past won't hurt so much.

God will walk by my side and again I will feel his touch.

Life plans can once again be made, dreams once more fulfilled,

daily living can carry on, the spirit no longer killed.

Life experiences will again have depth, feeling good will be the norm.

Energy consumed by our lament will take a different form.

Hope and joy will come again to fill our home once more

and songs of happiness and songs of love will issue from our door.

MY SOUL'S ON FIRE

God help me, my soul is on fire.
My heart labors beneath my breast.
I cannot understand what is going on,
is this some awful test?

What justice is there
when a child has to die;
the world is full of terrible people
why Lord, why my child, why?

The pain is so severe
I can think of none that is worse.
What has brought me to this day
what has sent this evil curse?

Is there no relief in sight?
We need to see and hear our son;
you sent us miracles before,
please send us another one.

MY DEAR WOUNDED CHILDREN
THE PAIN YOU FEEL IS REAL
YOU HAVE LOST A PART OF YOURSELF
THAT WILL TAKE A LONG TIME TO HEAL.

TAKE EACH MOMENT AS IT COMES
MOVE TO HOURS AND THEN TO DAYS
REMEMBERING YOU ARE STILL A FAMILY
CAN CUT THROUGH THE GRIEVING HAZE.

FIND STRENGTH IN EACH OTHER
YET FIND SPACE FOR YOURSELF TO GRIEVE
YOU ALL DESPERATELY NEED THE TIME
TO COMPREHEND AND TO BELIEVE.

BELIEVE HE IS IN A BETTER PLACE
BUT NOT TOTALLY OUT OF REACH
THERE ARE MANY AVENUES THAT CAN PROVIDE
PEACE AND GIVE RELIEF.

THE MIRACLES DO NOT STOP
BUT IN GRIEF THEY ARE HARDER TO SEE
THE PAIN DEADENS YOUR SENSES
BUT THEY ARE ALWAYS THERE FOR THEE.

REACH OUT TO YOUR SON

HE IS CLOSER THAN YOU THINK

OPEN UP YOUR SPIRITUAL EYES

AND YOU WILL FIND A LINK.

A PATH FOR YOUR HEALING

AND THE PLACE YOU NEED TO BE

SO YOU CAN SAY GOOD BYE

JUST ONE MORE TIME…

AND SET HIS SPIRIT FREE.

In memory of Bradley James Degraw

THIRD LETTER

June 25, 1988

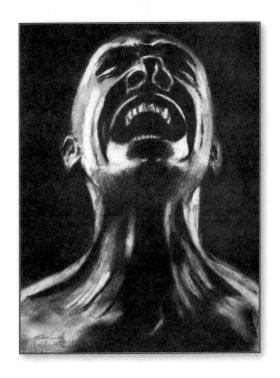

My heart is in anguish within me;

The terrors of death assail me.

Fear and trembling have beset me;

Horror has overwhelmed me.

I said, "Oh, that I had the wings of a dove!

I would fly away and be at rest."

—Psalm 55: 4–6

6-25-88
My dear son,

It has been one year ago this week that we were in Hawaii. I keep playing over and over in my mind our trip to paradise. I remember staying at the Diamond Head Beach Hotel where we sneaked up to the top and looked out over the city of Honolulu. Do you remember how scared you were of getting caught? I remember our first attempt at swimming at that not so nice beach near the hotel where the coral was so sharp, but we were excited to be in Hawaii. We later did stumble onto Waikiki beach and discovered how nice it was. Remember you and Meg getting a ride back in the little bike cart that a man was peddling? Mom and I waited back at the hotel for you.

I think of that sickening helicopter ride that you seemed to handle so well, despite that nasty tumor in your brain. I remember how you glowed in recognition and love for Walter, the Hawaiian that befriended you. I will never forget how he took you out by yourself snorkeling by the Capt. Cook Monument, while his girlfriend fed the fish from the boat. She was a hula dancer and how you loved the hula. You could not seem to get enough of it. I do not know how many shows we saw, but in every show you never missed a minute of it.

I think of you, my son, whenever I think of Hawaii and I think of Hawaii whenever I think of you . . . without fail. Do you remember the great time we had on the beach lighting the fireworks as you guys chanted like Indians? Then we all went skinny-dipping in the ocean at night. Wow what a blast that was. Crazy parents, huh?

I remember how cold you were at the Jessie Luau and you were wearing my shirt, but when Jesse called you up on the stage you took it off and proudly walked up there like you owned the place, and the last thing you looked like was cold. I get the chills still whenever I hear that song "Kanaka vi vi" that Jessie sang for you.

Kelly, I am so glad you wanted to go out and see Grandma and Grandpa Kuby before you died. We had such a great time out there. We did not do too much except watch movies and go for short walks and eat. Do you remember the old church down the hill that we investigated? I remember how you really were not feeling good when we went trout fishing, but you did it anyway for Grandma. I remember how you liked Grandma's friends because they had cats. I think you were missing Ernie.

I felt so bad for you when you were crying so hard for your mom when we first arrived and you couldn't stop whimpering. Then we started giving you a little bit of the magic morphine medicine that you grew to like. It took away the pains that you could not identify and relaxed you so not as many hot baths were necessary, considering their low water pressure and how long it took to fill the tub.

Remember, we could not find Cocoa Wheat's for love or money, and we invented our own with instant breakfast? That was the last time you saw your Grandma Kuby, She was so glad to have had that time with you. I remember all these times and I am happy that we had them, but I also remember that you were sleeping later and later every day. I would go in and check on you and listen for your breathing and check your heartbeat. I had no idea when you would be passing over, Kelly. There is no way to prepare for it, no way to know what to expect. These feelings got worse when we returned to that awful townhouse that we called home. I found myself ghoulishly checking on you at night to still see if you were alive. It was such a strange feeling, almost wanting to find you not breathing and have it all over with: your pain and mine.

When we had hope and we were filled with the spirit of survival and confronted every obstacle with a voracious desire to tear it down. There were no obstacles! During that last month that you were here with us, I lost all hope; I knew that it was over and you were returning home. I felt no fear checking on you or had no hopes that you would be alive. I knew death was coming and I almost ashamedly wished that it would just come and be all over with.

My only regret is not talking with you near the end that you were indeed dying. I truly believe that you knew and from a previous conversation I know you did not want to talk about dying. But I still wanted to talk to you about it and tell you, "Yes, Kelly, you are dying." You were so tired and listless and your breathing was erratic; we were not sure if you would be like this for weeks or not even last the day. We did not think it would be long, but yet really did not know. It hurts me so much when I think of you lying there on the couch fighting for your breath and staring off into the nothingness, so pale, so sad. I thank you for that wonderful smile that you left us with when you spirit left your body. That gave me the sign that you were now with God and your mission was complete.

Kelly I loved you as a son, I loved you as a boy, and I love you as you. But I never realized just how muchhhhh until now. I cannot believe how much it hurts. You remember in The Never Ending Story *movie there was "The Nothing." Well, when I am not hurting and not in unexpected bouts of normalcy, there is the ever constant, ever heavy nothing. A step out of place; a step out of time. So when the nothing gets to be too much, I remember, this brings the pain of your loss and the loss of your presence and this memory brings in the pain. I welcome it because with it your memory comes. If I cannot have you, then let me have the pain; it is all I have of you now. I cannot bear to walk by your picture sometimes and see nothing. A lot of the time, that is what I see … nothing and I know that helps to keep me in line with the rest of the world, everyday things to do, work, and of course taking care of Mom and Meg.*

Kelly I miss you and love you so much it is almost a physical concrete thing. At least as heavy as concrete and just as lasting. I dream of the day that we will again see each other when I leave this earth plane, or in my dreams. I thought things would be getting better and not worse. Right at this moment, I do not think I could feel your loss more profound. I want you back here with us! I want to watch you playing with your God damn Garbage Pail Kid cards; I want to see you teasing the shit out of Emily. I want to see you diving off the diving board. Christ, I want to see you graduate and have girlfriends. I want you!!!!!!!!

—Dad

This letter to Kelly was written six months following his death and I started replaying in my mind all the things we had done. The whole adventure of miracles and magic that had taken place in Mexico filled my thoughts. Did that all really happen? Did Kelly really sing in Spanish and swallow invisible pills? Did his tumor really disappear? Did we really sell all our belongings and our house and move to San Diego? Did we honestly set up our home as hospice and plan his funeral while he was still alive? These thoughts and more resounded through my head; it all sounded so crazy and unbelievable. But that is what happened, and it changed our lives forever.

You can imagine our pain and frustration when the cancer returned and killed him so quickly. We had experienced a miracle firsthand. Then where was our God? We had been so sure he was cured. Then Kelly's future was gone and my future with him in it was gone. Clinging to the mystery and magic of those days as well as our other journeys now consumed my every waking moment. Reflecting on our recent experiences, what we did and didn't do, brought back his memories, and with it the pain. With that pain a deep fury was also brought to the surface. The *anger* stage of bereavement reared its ugly head, and I was mad.

I would lash out at anybody for seemingly minor indiscretions. For a laid-back type of guy, this took many people by surprise. This was not in my nature, and I would always feel horrible afterward. There were a few exceptions, though that gave me pause. It seems when I "blew up" at a stranger that really (*in my estimation*) deserved a tongue lashing, I always felt better following the event. Anger and its umbrage of frustration needs to be released. Sometimes I would go out, deep into the woods, and just scream. One time I went to an abandoned auto junkyard and, with crowbar in hand, smashed dozens of headlights and windshields. But most of the time, I released my rage through my writing. This was evident in the last couple paragraphs in the previous letter and several of the poems that were written around the same time—all of which reflect my pain and longing.

Ah! Little at best can all our hopes avail us

To lift this sorrow, or cheer us, when in the dark,

Unwilling, alone we embark,

And the things we have seen and have known and have heard of, fail us.

—Robert Bridges
"On a dead child," stanza 7

Grief fills the room up of my absent child,

Lies in his bed, walks up and down with me,

Puts on his pretty looks, repeats his words,

Remembers me of all his gracious parts,

Stuffs out his vacant garments with his form.

—William Shakespeare

MAHALO SWEET HAWAII

Hawaii, land of sun and land of love
you call to me upon the breeze
o come and heal my son.

The rainbow o're the falls
scents of plumeria thick in the air
you call to me so gently
in my dark despair.

Sending messages of healing
of faith, hope and magic
with an awareness of God's presence
in a situation so tragic.

The pounding of the surf
and the swaying of the palm
massages mind and soul
with a tropical spiritual balm.

The warmth of the "Aloha"
the Hawaiian natural way
bathes the soul with healing
and troubles melt away.

The dawning of each new day
brings miracles in motion
with its warm tropic breezes
and salty smell of its ocean.

I pray to God every day
this healing will last
that Hawaii's magical blessing
will heal the hurts of past.

That my son will see the day
when we can make our return
to Hawaii and her islands
and the future that we yearn.

Mahalo sweet Hawaii
your touch I'll not forget
the magic of your people
we are forever in you debt.

GRACIAS A DIOS

Mexico you are a mystery, I'm not sure you will ever know
what kind of experience on us you did bestow.
We came here with open hearts as God lead the way;
leading us to our healing and our companion every day.

With your love and great goodness you brought hope to our door
bringing magic and compassion like never seen before.
We were brought down to reality, there was no time to waste
there were many things to be done and to do them in haste.

Kelly's body had to be restored, his energies increased,
many people were brought our way with what they had to teach.
They taught us of logic in the body's natural way
of healing its intrusions that beset us every day.

Restore the vital energies that medicines had absorbed
eating only natural food with a stronger faith in our Lord.
God had spoken to us and said our son was made whole;
that his healing was complete, and we had reached our prayed-for goal.

Instead of putting our son out to pasture and letting life take its course

we put our faith back in God, the power and the source.

Sometimes we tend to forget that God has set a plan

a course for all humanity, every woman and every man.

The course is never rigid, He helps us all the way,

we have to look for his guidance, giving thanks when we pray.

There is much power in collective prayer when their energies combine.

Sending waves of healing light down God's own power line.

We have received God's love through his sons and his daughters,

from the flora of the land, and its cleansing healing waters.

God has given back my son for he has many things to do

spreading the word of God's kindness … telling them of you.

HELPLESS TO THE MEMORIES

July 26,1988

Oh son, I miss you so with those hypnotic eyes of blue,
I long to hold you in my arms the way I use to do.
I crave to smell again the natural odor distinct to you
imprinted in my olfactory memory from the day that you were new.

I can still hear you giggle with that mischievous glint in your eye
squeezing the hell out of your hamsters or making your sister cry.
Swearing like a sailor with many things that you said
and how you loved to read the books that were stacked beside your bed.

Playing with your Garbage Pail Kid cards for hours on end
collecting every series they had with every dime that you could spend.
A day does not go by that I do not ruminate over my son
and I reflect upon my tragic loss and all the things that we had done.

I remember when this all began on that Sunday you saw double
and we raced to the hospital…we knew that you were in trouble.
Things have never been the same since that frightening day
when we found out you had cancer and our old lives were swept away.

Swept away and gone forever, there was no turning back
the perfect healthy family that we had, its future turning black.
Three brain surgeries later and a long hospital stay
we finally brought you home, how happy we were that day.

You were left very weak and partially paralyzed on one side
confined to a wheelchair, but had not lost your pride.
You were proud to be alive and glad to be at home again
trying to forget the pain and where you had been.

The wheelchair seemed fun at first but the novelty soon grew old
you realized your limitations before you were told.
You wanted badly to walk any way that you could
so with a tripod cane and some assistance you started doing good.

But soon you were embarrassed by the looks from your peers
and threw down the cane and with it your fears.
We watched you shuffle along holding on to the wall
biting onto our lips so afraid that you would fall.

Fall you did a couple of times and it made you very mad
the tears welled up in my eyes, I felt so very bad.
It hurt me to see you struggle so with your body so very weak
but you were so determined with every goal that you would seek.

So walk you finally did with patience, courage, and resolve

you overcame your obstacles and recovered from your falls.

You worked very hard with your therapist
and did everything she asked you to do,

she cared for you so very much and wanted to see you get through.

She pushed you pretty hard at times and you would get upset and cry

you were told it was for your own good, but hard to understand the why.

You switched the dominance of your hands now using your left instead of
your right

progressing very rapidly with your determination and your fight.

You wanted so very badly to again ride your bike down the street

but we were so very frightened of that potentially dangerous feat.

The back of your head was still healing, your neck was very stiff

balance and coordination a problem, leaving room for what if…

What if you fell on the sidewalk and hit your sensitive healing head

it wasn't so long ago you couldn't get out of bed.

But ride your bike you did, going round and round the block

your head held high and smiling… riding bike when
you could hardly walk.

The neighbors came out of their houses and they all cheered you on
Hip-hip hooray for Kelly Carmody and the victory he had won.
I will never forget that day and that **real** *smile on your face*
even though we had lost the war, we had won many a race.

I guess that is what hurts so much, to see all your efforts made in vain
all your courage and hard work, all the tears and all the pain.
You should have gotten more time for the steep price that you paid
experience more of life's happiness and plans that should be made.

That is my biggest regret that we did not have more time to share
with all the sacrifices you had made, it just wasn't fair.
Fair it may not have been but that is what transpired
the miracles had stopped and your time here expired.
I have to get used to the fact that you are really dead
that the life we had is over, except for re-runs in my head.
I am helpless to the memories, the good ones and the bad
that lay so close to the surface and make me feel so sad.

I just cannot get over you; I am not ready to put you away,
so I'll be self indulgent with my pain and think of you every day.
Yes it hurts so very much, and the pain may last for years
… but the pain is all that I have left, beside my daily tears.

FOURTH LETTER

September 8, 1988

Though they go mad they

shall be sane,

Though they sink through the sea

They shall rise again;

Though lovers be lost, love shall not;

And death shall have no dominion.

—Dylan Thomas (1936)

9-8-88
My Dearest son,

I think things are going better for us here at home. Better in comparison to where we have been, I guess is just a matter of intensity. I do not hurt, as deeply as before, or rather, I am not exhibiting as many painful manifestations as I have previously. I still think of you every day, almost the first thing in the morning and the last thing at night. As before it was almost nonstop thinking about you. There is probably nothing I do that I do not think about the activity in comparisons of with and without you.

This school year and beginning of school for Meagan seems so different without you. Your mother, who loved to shop with you so much and get you ready for school, is taking it pretty hard. You and she loved to go shopping and school was so important to you. Last year it was so strange with you kids starting school in a strange town and strange people. I hope we did not do wrong by you in doing what we did, but it seemed the right thing to do and you did seem strangely content in that school, compared to Meg who didn't like it at all. I am sorry I never picked up your erasures from that school. I remember fighting with the principal to let you ride your bike to school as well as the school nurse over shots for you. Some day we will talk it all over and we shall understand all the reasons and the whys.

Kelly, Meg is now playing T-ball and soccer and I support her and go to her games, but I cannot help feel a world apart from all the other parents and have no ambition to get involved. It makes me feel so sad thinking of all the things that you are missing out on. Even more so it makes me feel sad over missing out on seeing you involved in so many of life's experiences.

I truly do feel on a deeper soul level that you realized this experience was one of your choosing, for you own soul's reasons—Just as Jesus chose His path and knew of His certain demise. I am not saying He was ready to go easily but He knew what awaited Him. In the Garden of Gethsemane, He went through his personal turmoil just as you did when you found out your cancer was back. He knew that this was the end of His earthly life, but chose not to fight it anymore. The mission that He had to do was completed while still in the flesh. He did not rush to His death but accepted it as part of the plan. He did not really want to leave his earthly ties but did not resist, as He knew this is what He had chosen and what He had worked His whole life for.

Just as you worked your whole life to accomplish so much, in such little time. You had completed the task your soul had set forth in this life and when you innately knew it was over, you accepted it and went to meet your God. Jesus had personally met you two years earlier, floating above the operating table when he said, "You will be well." He had pulled you from the jaws of death, for your mission was not yet complete. The last two years are still trying to find a place in my reality and someday it will be a great story to move many people. Your life was truly an inspirational one and that is what gives me the strength to accept the unacceptable in human terms—your loss.

The state I am in now is hard to describe, but it is not the horrifying pain of before, but rather a strange indescribable state, which has followed a relatively up period. I am again finding meaning in life and look forward to utilizing all that you have taught me in your short life. My life has been profoundly changed and I am not who I used to be and I have plans for myself to be as good as I can be and help to heal this planet and its inhabitants.

I thank you for your great sacrifice and I hope I am worthy of carrying on the lamp of your illumination. I still miss you so much, and it hurts very *much if I dwell on it; so forgive me if I do not. I still love you with all my heart and soul and I will always be proud that you chose me as your father on this journey.*

With you always…Dad.

This, the fourth letter, nine months following Kelly's death, reflects a significant milestone in acceptance. By looking into the depth of destiny and recognizing that the flow of the universe is one of continual change, that energy does not dissipate, it only changes form. Growing from change is the opportunity we are presented with each and every day of our lives. We must seek from life's daily challenges the reasons that we are experiencing them.

When catastrophic change strikes, it is never more important to recognize how we can benefit our life, our family, and the world by experiencing this most difficult challenge. *Nothing* can be done to reverse what has happened. Death can be an angel in disguise for those in great pain; for them it is the ultimate cure. For those left behind, the only cure for the pain in grief is acceptance.

The key to acceptance of a significant death in your life is to experience the pain—never deny it. Play out the guilt, your shoulda, woulda, couldas, and let it go. We manufacture guilt and punish ourselves for things beyond our real control. We cannot control destiny, yet we can influence destiny by how we react. Every action causes a reaction. We can never change what has transpired, but we can influence what is yet to be. By choosing to go forward and using your pain to help alleviate pain in others, you will find that your pain is relieved in the process.

The heart has its reasons, which reason does not know.

—Blaise Pascal

GOLDEN OPPORTUNITY

Life is so full of pain, yet so full of light
the duality of our existence so apparent in my plight.
I intensely feel the pain of loss that will not go away
no matter how many books I read or hours that I pray.

They say that time heals all things but what else is there to say?
For time marches on, minute after minute, day after day.
There is no magic cure only a slow process of change
as our perceptions of reality grows more lucid and less strange.

The pain never really goes away, a lesson we are cruelly learning
but lies in a state of remission; a glowing ember always burning.
It is in understanding this lesson that we gain some relief
we don't shut out our loved one's life but hold on to our belief.

Our belief that life never really dies and we shall be together again
and understand that this present moment will too have an end.
The only constant we have is change and change is the essence of being
a metamorphic blueprint in flux that we resist our minds from seeing.

Man is resistant to life's modulations forever clinging to the past,

wanting things the way they were
and for the present moment to forever last.

That can never happen, we cannot hold back tomorrow

for the sun will surely rise and with it, pain and impending sorrow.

So we must look for the gift encapsulated in our grief

seek out the potential for growth and what the experience has to teach.

There is no way to change the fact that our loved one has died

no miracle that can bring them back or erase the tears that we have cried.

We must face the cold reality that a part of us is gone forever

the physical evidence of their existence cut from our parental tether.

The awful truth of our loss makes us escape inside

cut off from the rest of the world, a safe place to hide.

And hide we must to endure the pain,

a time to recharge the spirit and not go insane.

But after a period of time we have to break out

or lose touch with the world and what we're about.

We have the golden opportunity to advance our spiritual being

and turn sorrow to joy; a different perspective in our seeing.

Seeing the potential in all life experience that can fortify our soul

bringing us closer to God and the healing of humanity our goal.

To transcend our painful condition that man is reticent to communicate

and make their life a legacy that through our acts can illuminate.

If we can use the energy consumed in our bereavement

and transform it into a tool for our own spiritual achievement.

If we can only give credence to their life;
that there was a reason they chose this path

and that their soul had chosen this direction
and not some vengeful God's wrath.

That we as family were also selected to assist them on their way

players in a greater plan we shall too understand some day.

So we must try to make the best of a clearly unacceptable situation,

and put our self-pity to a rest and grow in spiritual maturation.

Our lives will never be the same without them at our side,

but what a gift they have given us, their love…that in us will always reside.

IN THE SHADOW OF MY DESPAIR

You have no idea just how I feel
unless you're in my shoes
no way you can comprehend
the depth of sorrow in my blues.

The shock carried me away
when my son first died
a cloud like calm enveloped me
as friends hugged me and we cried.

They then felt the bitter pain
putting themselves in my place
envisioning the loss of their child
as they gazed upon his face.

They at once realized how vulnerable
one can truly be
how painful that reality
was brought clear for them to see.

To see such a beautiful child
laying cold and lifeless in his funeral bier
strikes terror in any parent's heart
that their child could too expire.

Uncomfortable people don't know what to say
so you hear, "If there is anything that I can do…."
feeling helpless in a situation
so difficult to get through.

So many people often exclaim,
"I don't know how you do it,
I love my children so awfully much
there is no way I could get through it."

My God! Does this mean because I am calm,
I love my children less?
How else could I handle it,
under such great duress.

God grants us a little time
a short period that we are numb with shock
to attend to funereal arrangements
and the ability to even talk.

It is when the wake is over
the funeral said and done
the graveside interment finished
or the ashes scattered in the sun.

These acts of life's finality
start to erode the façade of calm
and the reality of my great loss
breaks down God's numbing balm.

It is said that grief takes time
at least two years most experts agree
before a semblance of normalcy
will start to return to me.

At times I feel quite normal
in fact almost good
and then the boom is lowered
as I expected that it would.

Intense pain then returns
and racks my very soul
depression I have never know before
starts to take its toll.

The real world fades away...
people talk and are not heard
apathy surrounds my being
it's difficult to utter a word.

Tears flow in a sudden flood
with deep convulsive groans
wails of torment escape my throat
that vibrate from my bones.

As an exhausted shell of myself
I feel washed out and spent
the intensity diminishing
from this scenario of my lament.

I slowly then recover
and feeling better in part
it seems a great weight has been lifted
temporarily from my heart.

It is these intense feelings
other people do not perceive,
not realizing the profundity of pain
that each day I do receive.

Their lives go on as before
with a modicum of change
their petty priorities seem unimportant
that in their lives they do arrange.

I have a lowered tolerance
for trivial problems that people exclaim
no time for their trifling complaints
or who won the baseball game.

I understand that it is my perception
it is no fault of their own
but I cannot help the way I'm feeling
caught in this "grieving zone."

I wonder how long it will take
before I lose a friend
because of my intolerant moods
that could put a friendship to end.

I think that friends that truly care
will always be by my side
and in the shadow of my despair
their love will reside.

It may take several years
before I can stand tall again
and I will thank God for the loving arms
of the people I still call friends.

O Death the healer, scorn thou not, I pray

To come to me: of cureless ills

thou art the one physician.

Pain lays not its touch upon a corpse.

—Aeschylus (456 BC)

FIFTH LETTER

October 31, 1988

> *Hearts that are united through the medium of sorrow,*
>
> *Will not be separated by the glory of happiness.*
>
> *Love that is cleansed by tears will remain eternally pure and beautiful…*

—KAHIL GIBRAN

10-31-88

My Dearest son,

Here it is Halloween again, your holiday of all holidays, but this year it is not the same and it will be quite awhile before it ever is again. I remember how excited you would get and how you would talk about your new costume months before Halloween; those years in Bayport, when things were normal and you were well. You and your buddy Jason would hit the streets, bags in hand…ahhhh, those were the days.

Last year I was in California all by myself, while you, Meg and your mom were back in Minnesota making the rounds of your last Halloween. Your mom told me how you crawled up to a few doors because you were too weak to walk. It breaks my heart to think about it, but it showed your determination and priorities.

Kelly, it has been a roller coaster of emotions since you died. I thought it was getting better; then two weeks ago the bottom fell out of my reality and I lapsed into a period of deep depression. I called in sick to work, as I was truly out of it. I immersed myself into you for days. I watched all the home movies/videos and looked at photos and I cried. I miss you so much that I tried to occupy my thoughts with busy activities or deaden the pain with alcohol. At times I feel like a wounded dog running away for his pain and being unable to, I finally collapse into an exhausted heap.

This last spell was by far the worst and lasted almost a week. I know it will not be the last, but God help me, it wiped me out. When I came out of it, I felt much better and still feel good, except for the fact now of Halloween. With your upcoming birthday, death day, and Christmas I feel very vulnerable. I feel so confused trying to sort it all out and maintain a normal life. It is hard to feel normal when every thought or action that I have is filtered through the grieving me. Every quark of my being is in grief.

All input is only relevant as it is seen without you. It's like seeing life on a television screen that has severe weather warnings flashing constantly on the bottom of the screen: "WARNING! KELLY IS DEAD. HOW CAN YOU VIEW THE WORLD NORMALLY WITH THIS KNOWLEDGE?" Right now it feels as if this storm warning will be with me the rest of my life; at this point, I just don't know. I thought I had all the answers in dealing with death and dying, but I found out there really are no pat answers. Someday I will join you and then, I too, shall know.

Remember when I asked you to give me a sign this spring of something new growing in our yard? Thank you for responding with the three cornstalks. I know it was you that sent them. Three cornstalks growing right out of the lawn, now that is quite a trick!!! I think the first stalk represented the birth and death of your life before cancer. The second stalk, the symbol of your healing and your ultimate physical death. The third stalk survived and bore three ears of corn that bore the fruits of seeds you had sown. The first two corn stalks died as did your body and mind. The third lived and bore fruit as your spirit also lives and is now bearing fruit for all to see. One ear was for Meg, one ear for your mom, and one for me. We shall treasure them. It is also interesting to let you know that Meg came home with a book from the school library called The Three Corn Stalks. *The book indicates that the three stalks are an ancient sacred symbol for Mexico. I thought the reason you chose the cornstalks had something to do with Mexico.*

I promised you that I would quit smoking last January 1st and I did. I feel that was another gift from you. You are no longer here in the physical, but you continue to affect change in my life. So in my mind, part of you is still very much alive, more than just the eternal spirit living on aspect, but a real living spark of who you are, still lives on in my soul. This is whom I am writing to.

Your legacy is also alive and growing and someday I shall finish the book of your life and our adventure. It will give to the world an example of what great love and faith in God can do. I am proud to be a small part in bringing it to the world. Through your struggle and suffering others shall find hope and in finding hope, find and know their God. I thank you again for choosing me as your dad, that fact alone helps me bear the pain and continue on with my life. Together we shall spread the word, as was prophesied last summer in Mexico.

I love you and miss you desperately. I long for your touch that I cannot do a damn thing about, which is so painfully frustrating. As I was tickling Meg last night, I tried to remember the last time I actually tickled you and you laughed a deep hearty child's laugh. It was a long time ago. You had to grow up so fast and give up so much before you ever left us physically;

for that I am sorry. This path was your choice, just as Jesus chose his path.
The sufferings known here on earth are nothing compared to the great
joy that you are now experiencing in the bosom of our God. Until I write
again … its hello and not goodbye.

—Dad

This letter was written on Halloween night, eleven months after Kelly's death. It vividly reflects the rollercoaster of emotions that one can experience in the process of their grief. Special days and holidays are especially difficult in the first year without your loved one. Last year they were still alive and together you were making memories of every special moment for the last time. This year they are but a memory.

There will be times that you will want to immerse yourself into the memories and feel the pain. Recognize the pain and the emotions that come with it; allow it all in. Bittersweet emotions will well up and you will feel vulnerable and alone. This can be difficult, but it is very therapeutic, as it allows vivid recollections involving all of your senses. In this space and time you become very close to your loved one and can actually feel the closeness of their spirit. This is the joy that lies beneath the pain, the gift in the grief, a taste of their life, be it ever so brief. Do not put away their memories forever; let them help heal and nourish your spirit. As Frederic Nietzsche said, "That which does not kill me, makes me stronger."

Take a chance. It may be difficult and exhausting, but it's worth the price. You get so much back, and it can actually be a stimulus for your healing. Be open to signs from your loved one; it is at these especially painful times that they reach out to us in our need. It may be a song on the radio, a bird at the windowsill, their scent on the wind, or a very vivid dream—a seemingly insignificant random event occurring at just the right time.

This letter is again about total acceptance; about hitting the nadir of pain and depression by immersing yourself into the pain; about feeling it all, then slowly getting up and accepting the future, as it is, your life without them—they are dead. Our family, our jobs, the world, needs us back with them. We have to continue on with our good works that we have yet to manifest and pursue the path that God has set before us. We will be provided with the strength when we need it the most. We have many lives that we have yet to influence, hearts to touch, and souls that need to connect. This is our destiny, and we have to play it out and grow from it however it presents itself.

Look for the design in our experiences that can influence our choices in the future. There are no accidents, no mistakes, and no poor choices; there is only acceptance of *all* the choices you have made. The magic of it is…we always have choices—and it's always the right choice for us. This may be difficult to understand soon after experiencing the effects of a perceived poor choice (real or imagined), but it is those effects that we experience that pave the way to our future. Pitfalls can be windfalls; roadblocks can be stepping-stones; and the Y in the road will always rise up to meet us.

> *Our destiny exercises its influence over us even when,*
> *as yet, we have not learned its nature: it is our future*
> *that lays down the law of our today.*
>
> —Friedrich Nietzsche

FOOTSTEPS THROUGH THE VALLEY OF THE SHADOW OF DEATH

Yea as I walk through the valley of the shadow of death

bearing the burden of grief upon my back.

The valley is dark, deep and suffocating—

I long for the fresh air that I lack.

The journey into the valley is a lonely one,

neither is it night, nor is it day,

it is not hot and dry, cold and wet

only different shades of gray.

The walls of the valley are spongy and thick
they seem to absorb all sound.
The floor has a great gravitational pull
making it difficult to get around.

Time stands still in this awful place
a direction is hard to find;
one wanders aimlessly about
in a dreamlike state of mind.

The air is dense and viscous
almost liquid as it surrounds your being.
When you try to reach out to a friend
it occludes your eyes from seeing.

It seems there is no escape,
no possible place to run.
You long to find an open door
that will again let in the sun.

You raise your hands up to God
to beseech Him for a healing.
Begging Him to take away your pain
and the emotions you are feeling.

Your supplications seem to fall on deaf ears,
God apparently is not around.
Maybe He is off helping others
unaware of your lamenting sounds.

It is now that you really need Him
to rescue you from this desolate concavity.
Craving the comfort of His embrace
and away from death's depravity.

Where is my God; now tell me;
why is there no answer to my call?
have years of faith deserted me
now that my back is to the wall?

I know that death is our greatest reward
the overlying reality that is in store.
Knowing that death is a but a mere transition
an altered state but yet so much more.

This is of course, is the Nirvana of Heavenly glory
for those who leave the human plane
But does little for the survivors
that are left alone and racked with pain.

For we are the ones who are left to die
in the valley of the shadow of death
To perish when our day too will come
and we draw our final breath.

It may seem that God has forsaken us
as we travel alone in this canyon of despair
—But it is then that He carries us
and was and will always be there.

It is just that in our pain
it is hard to feel His hand.
So He carries us ever so gently
until again we can finally stand.

Stand up to the stark reality
of the loss that we have to bear.
Realizing we must live our lives to the fullest
with the love we have yet to share.

So if you feel God has abandoned you
in the depths of your deepest sorrow.
Remember God always listens,
and will be there for you tomorrow.

Soul Talk

—Meagan Carmody (Kelly's sister)

As I live my life, I see, hear, and feel things
which is all for the "soul" purpose of me experiencing this life.
My mission in this life is to try to live to the fullest.
To learn and understand my deck of cards that lay out before me to play.

There will be good cards and there will be bad,
both of which I will have to deal with.
I believe God has sent me on this journey to teach me lessons
of which I have not yet acknowledged from my past lives.

I will try to understand everything that God will allow my soul to learn.
So far my journey has been about understanding loss and the grief of
losing a loved one, how you find your inner strength to help you accept
how death can be beautiful if you let it.

I have learned of pain and suffering of war and how cruel
people can be to each other.
If only people would listen to their souls and look into their dreams. I know
love can overcome everything in life no matter what the situation.

I am the protector of my family in this lifetime.

I'm here to be their strength and the sole core

which holds these two beautiful people together.

God gave me that gift. I truly believe that I was born

by this couple to help guide them through their life

as they are helping me get to know and experience my life as a beautiful

thing, and how love can overcome…Everything.

Oh, call my brother back to me!

I cannot play alone:

The summer comes with flower and bee … Where is my brother gone?

—Felicia Dorthea Hemans

SIXTH LETTER

December 25th, 1988

Things do not change; we change.

—Henry Thoreau (*Walden*, 1854)

12-25-88
Dear Kelly,

Well, today is Christmas Day, and it is just not the same without you. I love Christmas songs and the general atmosphere of Christmas, but now that it is here I feel quite miserable and miss you more than ever. It is important that we keep our chins up for Meagan because Christmas is for kids after all. But this is a chore!!!! I feel so tired and it is not just the midnight shift. My throat has a lump in it that seems worse on that shift, when I am so tired. The doctor says it is stress and recommended Valium. I refuse to be put on Valium forever so I will try to live with it and keep my stress level down. Maybe all my losses have finally caught up to me, with your loss being the straw that broke the camel's back. Sometimes I wish the world would stop and let me off. How long am I going to feel this way? There are worse disasters, more carnage in the world than I have experienced. Why can't I feel better when I rationalize this way?

Remember last February when I asked you for a sign growing in the yard this spring? I never in my wildest dreams thought that you could orchestrate such a profound message as you did. Yes, I found the three cornstalks growing in the yard. I understand they represent the healing that took place in Mexico. I was happy with just the presence of the cornstalks, but ecstatic and overjoyed with the message you sent to that last ear of corn on December 1, with the one word "DAD" written in the husk with corn mold for ink... Wow! How astounding! I lived on that for weeks.

I am sure you saw how we were on the anniversary of your death. I have never cried so much and so hard in my life. I cannot believe how much it hurt that day. I guess I fully realized that you were dead and let myself truly feel that all day long. I know now it is going to take a long, long time to heal. I never knew I could love somebody so much. I have never known depression before or had any stress related illness. I understand that by the nature of things I will get better, but maybe I don't want to just yet. I just do not know!

I know that the holidays would be rough and we shall see how we recover. Thank you for the energy that you expended to get back to me. I will love you all the rest of my days. When you have the strength, please give Dustin a visit. He is hurting pretty bad still. I will try to help from this end…Always loving you my dear, sweet son.

—Dad

This sixth letter clearly illustrates the pain and sadness experienced during the holidays and the anniversary date. Conversely it also reflects the joy that is received from miracles of the spirit, undying love, and faith.

As I wrote in this letter, I was experiencing physical symptoms from my grief. The pain on his death day anniversary was extreme and profound. We opened his trunk of things containing drawings, toys books, Garbage Pail Kid cards, the blanket he died in and lots of nine-year-old boy stuff. We immersed ourselves into the pain and cried deep, wailing and painful tears.

In the first letter, I had asked Kelly to get back to somebody with the *code word*. When Kelly was still alive, his mom had talked to Kelly about dying, and together they had come up with a code word. Kelly promised her that, if he died, he would get back to her with their code word. After we had gone through all the stuff in Kelly's trunk and were putting things back, we found an old notebook in a pile of his magazines. It looked unused with little or no writing in it, but when we were

putting it back into the trunk it fell open to one page with a single drawing on it. The drawing was one of those simple kid drawings where you
trace out your hand and make a turkey, and it had the letters of Kelly's
name on each finger. The code word had been turkey. Another coincidence? Maybe. But we knew better, and our spirits were again lifted.
We were emotionally spent and exhausted, yet buoyed with gifts from
the spirit.

At that time, I was experiencing some tightness in my throat, which
felt like a huge lump, making it difficult to swallow. My doctor could
find nothing physically wrong and thought it might be stress related
(imagine that). I quit drinking coffee and tried to reduce other stress-
ors in my life. The doctor now wanted to try Valium, but I did not want
to medicate my pain. The reason for the pain, I believed, was from my
current, horrific grief on top of old, unexpressed grief that needed to be
released.

I now sought a more holistic approach, and with the new age thinking paradigm shift in full swing, there were many avenues to explore. I
had experienced the rebirthing process for the first time when we were
in California and was impressed with its results. I searched locally and
soon found a lady who practiced the process out of her home in Wisconsin. I thought, if I went back to day one, I might find some clue to
help me now. I made an appointment, since the throat thing was driving me crazy.

I drove to her house in rural Wisconsin with cautious optimism.
The woman was very earthy (people I chidingly call "granola eaters")
and in her late fifties. The house was quiet with no one else apparently
there. She took my coat and hat and brought me down to her studio in
the basement. She had me lie down on a couch while she sat next to
me on a hardback chair holding my hand. She slowly explained to me
about rebirthing and what I was to expect. I was told to breathe very
slowly, relax, clear my mind and concentrate only on my breathing. As

I was getting my rhythm down, she explained that I might or might not go back to the day of my birth. What happened would be what was supposed to happen for me, and that could mean going back to any significant event in my life.

I kept up my rhythmic breathing as she sat quietly by my side, coaching occasionally when my rhythm would stray. I then heard the furnace kick on in the next room, and I was immediately launched back to the day my father died. I was fourteen years old, in my bed in a basement room next to the furnace. It was early morning, and I had to get up to get ready for the county fair to exhibit my dog for a 4-H project. My father was in the hospital, recovering from triple bypass surgery; my mother, who had been there all night, had just gotten home. She called me upstairs and said, "Son, you are the man of the house now. Your father has died, and we need to tell your sisters."

I then started to cry, harder and harder, and screamed loudly, "NO!!!" at the top of my lungs, probably scaring the wits out of this poor lady. Her gentle touch and soothing voice brought me back to reality. I was back in *her* basement on her couch, on a pillow wet with tears, the pain in my throat worse than ever. I tried to regain my composure; it was as if I had suddenly awakened from a very vivid dream. The epiphany then hit me, and I realized that I was never allowed to grieve for my father. My mother's words, "You are the man of the house now," came back to me. I then understood what I had done at such a young age. I had taken on the role. I had been the man of the house and had taken care of what needed to be done. There was no more grieving; I solicitously put it away and took care of the house, the farmyard, my mom, and my sisters.

I left rural Wisconsin that day feeling weird, tired, apathetic, sad, depressed, with a sore throat worse than when I had arrived. My head was filled with thoughts of my father—everything about him. I could even smell his scent right there in the car. Most of these strong recollections faded within a few days and, to my delight, so did the lump in my throat. I surmised that, before I could adequately deal with my present grief and pain for my son, I had needed to go back and deal with the unresolved grief for my father. It had worked!

As I stated earlier, there was a miracle of the spirit that happened on Kelly's death day anniversary: the miracle of the cornstalks. These miracles happen all around us every day, all the time. It is our perception and our faith that allows us to see them. You do not have to be psychic, clairvoyant, or clerical leader to experience these phenomena; the ability lies within us all and is closer to the surface than you think. Participating in a miracle also has an analgesic affect that helps heal the spirit in the process of bereavement. When I had asked my son for a sign from the grave that he was doing fine, I never dreamed something so profound and miraculous could happen. The poem that follows tells the story, but sufficed to say, it was a miracle. This for me was when the true healing began, bringing with it acceptance and letting go.

The Miracles of the Church seem to me to rest not so much upon faces of or voices or healing power coming suddenly near to us from afar off, but upon our perceptions being made finer, so that for a moment our eyes can see and or ears can hear what is there about us always.

—Willa Sibert Cather

THE THREE CORN STALKS

In December of last year

my young son passed away

I wanted proof that he survived

so I would talk, when I did pray.

I asked him for a sign

that would grow in our yard this spring

not a timely rainbow

or a bird on a wing.

I requested a living indication
that Kelly would manifest
growing from God's green earth
a portent at my request.

That summer we had a drought
the ground as dry as bone
but yet from the parched and dried up lawn
three plants grew all alone.

Three corn stalks grew
where none had grown before
no seeds were ever planted
amongst the weeds galore.

These three corn stalks formed a triangle
its terminus pointing southwest
toward the land of Kelly's healing
and the miracle that we knew best

Later in the summer
the northwest corn stalk withered and bent
like the loss of Kelly's childhood
before his life was spent.

A few weeks later
the northeast corn stalk died
just as Kelly's physical body had
where his soul had chosen to reside.

The last corn stalk survived
and bore fruit for all to see
a sacred symbol of Mexico
are the corn stalks three.

This year on the first of December
a mourning dove sat at our door
beseeching us to watch her
for the message that she bore.

This bird captivated us
as she hopped across the lawn
then flew over the lone corn stalk
and in a moment…was gone.

I trudged through the snowy yard
anticipation thick in the air
my intuitive senses reeling
in hopes of what could be there.

I examined the dried and withered stalk
for a message it might contain
and near the bottom nearly covered with snow
one last ear did remain.

I plucked this last and lonely ear
pulling its yellowed husk slowly back
within I found a tiny cob
with mold of green and black

This putrefaction of the cob
imprinted a word that could be read
stained clearly on the yellow husk
the word DAD ... *was all it said.*

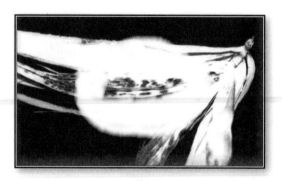

LOVE ME, NEVER LEAVE ME

My God I need your presence
like I never have before
my healing is slow and painful
with memories behind every door.

This time of year
will never be the same
for my family and for the many friends
of my dear son who was slain.

The summer is beginning
young graduates are everywhere
Tunes of pomp and circumstance
ring loudly in the air.

Commencement ceremonies carry on
as my tears flow in streams
proud parents unaware
of my pain of unrealized dreams.

Unaware of my inner pain
that sears the soul in grief
mourning for the life of my son
whose time here was much too brief.

His physical life was removed
stolen from me in his prime
never to know his kiss again
or feel his love sublime.

I feel so damn cheated
A deep sadness covers my heart
please let the time pass quickly
and I can make another start.

Start my second year of healing
learning to live again
to climb through this fog of sorrow
and where my life has been.

I forgive my son for dying
I will let his spirit fly
release the anger still in my heart
no longer asking why.

I know there are no answers
that I can and will endorse
my life goals have now been changed
on a totally different course.

I know not where I am going
so God please lead the way
help me again find the strength
to greet another day.

Hold on to me dear Lord
wrap me in your loving arms
I feel so alone and helpless
life has lost all its charms.

I know countless others
who have also endured this pain
their sons and daughters lost in war
or cancerous cells gone insane.

No matter when our children are taken
it will always be unfair
when they depart this earth before us
and leave us in dark despair.

So grant me Lord

those special moments that only you can give

that can alleviate my sorrow

and I can begin again to live.

To live my life in its altered course

and do the things that I can

just being able to function at all

is proof that you have a plan.

So God, love me never leave me

I need you everyday

I feel your loving presence

whenever I sit and pray.

And when I pray to you my Lord

I feel Kelly's presence in my heart

thank you for that gift

and the peace that it imparts.

SEVENTH AND LAST LETTER

April 2, 1989

> *I have no pain, dear mother, now;*
>
> *But oh! I am so dry:*
>
> *Just moisten my poor lips once more;*
>
> *And, mother, do not cry!*
>
> —Edward Farmer

4-2-89
My dearest son,

I have not written for quite awhile, but I think that means I am doing better. The signs that you have given us have been truly miraculous and I share them with many people. When you sent the five doves when I was reading the poem Letting Go to your mother was awesome! You know me well enough to find out what the significance of the number five was. I talked to a lady at church who was a numerologist and she said it meant, "Letting go!!!" My God that says it all.

I take that sign as a mutual letting go as we release each other to move on. I still would like to hear from you now and then although. I would really like to have a heart to heart talk with you as visually as you can make it (or I can make it) or better yet as we can both make it in my dreams. I need one good last hug from you that will last me for the rest of my life. I miss you so much!!!!! I miss you like you have just gone away and my heart aches at certain times that just pop up. It is not the intense pain that it was. There is the pain of separation, being away from you physically. Then there is the pain of separation itself, the actual act of separation that was so intense and painful. That separation has finally reached its breaking point and the separation has taken place. Now it is just the ache of our being separated and not the extreme pain of the separation process.

Just as your mother raised you for nine months inside her womb, nurturing you and protecting you, she then had to give you up after the ninth month. She had to separate from you physically and it was very painful, that act of separation. She then suffered later after she recovered with the ache of that separation. She no longer was physically responsible for your life, and she felt the loss of the ultimate maternal feeling of having you inside of her and grieved that. Now after nurturing you and being responsible for you for nine years, she then had to give you up again, and with it came that terrible pain of separation. The whole separation scenario played over again. Only this time, you are now born into a new life that is a more permanent separation. There is no physical contact. It may be a quick return for you, but a long wait for us until we can see you again.

Our return to Mexico was of great importance for us all. It gave us an opportunity to let go and carry on with our personal destinies. We cannot change the facts of our separation so we must make the best of where we are now. For a while, I just wanted to die and join you, while selfishly ignoring all the responsibilities I have here, especially for your sister. I also now realize what a great legacy you left us with, and I would be renege in my duty not to carry on the work that you had started. The work and purpose of your lifetime was the main reason that we were picked as your parents by you. You picked us to help in the task set before you and to carry on with your work and the work of our Lord's that now seems so synonymous in their natures.

If I was to give up and become an emotional cripple and let the pain of separation maim me for life, I would be doing you such a great disservice and make your life of great trials and tribulations all for naught. I must and will spread the word of God and what faith in him can do and I shall do it my son, with your life. Not many people have done as much with their life at full measure as you have done already with your few short years on this earth. We will continue on with our path that you have started for us. I feel more abundant in the spirit than ever before in my life. You've given that to me, Kelly, and I thank you. I want to be of service to mankind and my God more than ever before.

I would give it all up in a heartbeat if I could only have you back here with us, but that can never be, so I will expand upon all that we have learned in the school that was your life. I will help to heal mankind as best I can and spread the word of the faith that can produce miracles. You will always *be an active part of my life and together we shall turn my sorrow into joy. Please continue to be that light that guides me and keeps my spirit alive and let me be a conduit of healing energy.*

As man suffers at the thought of the crucifixion of Christ, and yet without that reality that he knew was his destiny, where would the world be today? Just as you did, knowing your destiny would create a living testimony of faith. We suffer at our loss, but rejoice in the glory that is your spirit.

I love you,
—Dad

This was the last letter that I had penned to my son, some fifteen months down the road following his death. It was then that I finally accepted the fact that he was really dead. Part of that acceptance had to deal with a trip back to Mexico. My wife thought it was crazy, but she acquiesced at my insistence that it was something we needed to do.

So much magic happened in Mexico, and we as a family were buoyed up spiritually from the whole experience. Then a year and some months following his death, I had to go back to Mexico and see if it had all been real. The memory of it all seemed like some vivid dream that I could not let go of. Return we did, only to find a whole different landscape.

The beach house where we had stayed for several months had burned to the ground. Nothing remained. We went to the chapel where the healing had taken place. Doña Nieves, who owned the chapel, was in Mexico City for an extended stay and was not available. The medium (Maria) had not been around for quite some time we were told. We did not meet any of the friends that we had made, and we were even hassled by the local police.

When we had been there before, we were treated like gods, and everyday was a good day. It was as if it had all been a dream, like a *Brigadoon* experience that was there for a short time, only to vanish again. We drove that day out of Mexico with very mixed emotions. We knew the miracles had happened. How could it have all changed so much? What did it all mean?

We flew home, and when the plane pulled onto the runway and up to the terminal, I received my answer. I could see my wife's parents in the window holding the hand of our daughter Meagan. It was then that I realized that she was all I had left. She deserved all of me. As I stared at Meagan, I had a vision, a mental image of my son's face on a large kite in the vast blue sky. His eyes were alive, happy and as brilliantly blue as the sky around him. His smile was one of peace, contentment, and self-realized assuredness. Gazing into his eyes once more, I found myself lost in a reverie of pure joy. With tears streaming down my face and totally unaware of my surroundings, I saw myself clutching desperately to the string that connected to the kite. It was then that I realized how extremely tight I was holding on to the string. I was so afraid of letting it go.

Momentarily, my connection to the outside world returned, and as if looking through a tunnel I stared at my darling daughter behind the thick safety glass. I then knew I had to make a choice to let go of my son and give all my energy to my daughter, who was alive and needed me so much. It was painful for me to do it, but as I slowly walked up the ramp to my awaiting daughter, I unclenched my hand and let go of the kite string. The kite never strayed but remained high in the azure sky, and my son smiled down at me as if to say, "Now that wasn't too hard was it, Dad?" My daughter was then running down the ramp, and soon was wrapping her arms around me. I scooped her up in an instant, holding her very tight. I gave Kelly a wink, the vision fading as I covered my daughter with tender kisses. It felt good to come home.

From wind to wind, earth has one tale to tell;

All other sounds are dulled, and drowned, and lost,

In this one cry "farewell."

—Celia Laighton Thaxter

LETTING GO ...

We embraced a miracle
that not long ago cured our son
his malignant brain tumor disappeared
and we no longer had to run.

We had traveled down to Mexico
after two weeks in the Hawaiian Isles
with the enchantment of that paradise
still evident in our smiles.

My son was feeling better
our daughter was having a ball
my wife and I just happy
to be away from it all.

To be away from our jobs
no television, movies, or phones
no well-meaning surprise visits
we were very much alone.

We ate up the sun and beach
consumed healthy foods everyday
as a family we were truly one
giving thanks to God as we prayed.

In this little Mexican village
we were guided to a chapel
and the Lord spoke to us of a healing
without radiation, drugs, or scalpel.

Jesus announced through this old woman
that our son would be healed
with diet, lots of faith, and a little magic
his death sentence could be repealed.

Raw eggs still in the shell
were rubbed upon his head
surgery in pantomime performed
by a doctor who was dead.

A doctor who in spirit
dispensed medications from thin air
changing spiritual bandages daily
we believed that he was there.

My son could see and feel
the invisible pills he was asked to take
we felt the presence of the Lord
with each appearance He would make.

It was spoken that he would be well
in just six weeks time
we followed the spiritual instructions
in hopes that he would be fine.

My son started singing in fluent Spanish
an ancient hymn out of the blue
sung in harmony with the Mexican locals
—it was then that we knew.

Knew that God had lead us here
to this remote little town
being coworkers in a miracle
in an experience so profound.

We put our lives on hold
as a family we were together
we put all our faith in God
and enjoyed the beach and sunny weather.

The real world had stopped
and we gladly got off for awhile
to totally work on our son's healing
and again see his radiant smile.

Our son's strength progressively returned
he could run and swim again
we could see him change before our very eyes
from the sick boy he had been.

In the little chapel it was said my son was healed
take him back to your doctors at home
and prove to them what God has done
with the faith that you have shown.

The doctors were totally shocked
they could not believe their eyes
the MRI scan showed no tumor
that previously was baseball size.

We danced on air that day
with smiles that couldn't fade
the greatest feeling in all my life
the sweetest victory ever made.
Circumstances changed in the months that followed
and dark clouds returned our way
my son's cancer spread like fire
our victory was turning gray.

My boy's spirit left his body
his physical journey here ended
to join with his God & maker
on whose miracle we had depended.

We put our faith in God
and He allowed the final healing
I was grateful for my son's peace
but hard to comprehend the pain that I was feeling.

The extreme pain lasted a long time
I grieved so very hard
still crying in anguish a year later
or whenever I was caught off guard.

My wife and I decided to return
to Mexico and its magic
say goodbye to all that it held
and the joy that turned so tragic.

The beach home where we had stayed
had mysteriously burned to the ground
the homes on either side
left unscathed and standing sound.

The chapel was quiet and empty
our hearts were filled with sadness
had the miracle really happened
or was this all sheer madness?

It was as if though
we were never there
just a little village in Mexico
with the smell of salt sea air.

We had lived a Brigadoon existence
the reality is what we made it
the miracle could have happened anywhere
on any stage that we had played it.

There is no going back
what was, will never be
we had been blessed by God
and now what was … is free.

When the plane landed on the runway
I could feel my daughter's heart
through the hard steel and heavy glass
I felt the love it did impart.

I knew right at that moment
she was our whole family now
a new life built for her
that we will endorse and allow.

When my son went to spirit
I held his soul like a kite
afraid to let go of the silver string
lest his soul would soar out of sight.

In my mind, I let go of that string
his face still smiling down at me
it was in the letting go
that set my spirit free.

My son will always be there
I did not need to hold on so tight
now I can grasp on to other things
and still behold his loving light.

We experienced a powerful miracle
feeling God's love in manifest
something I shall remember always
but yet can put to rest.

Be put to rest as my past
but still be shared will all
giving a legacy to his life
as he answered to his call.
I loved my son very dearly

and miss him with all my heart
but by letting him move on
my new journey will begin to start.

—a new beginning 3-3-89

Following Your Bliss through Despair

Why am I surrounded in pain that others never see;

some people seem protected from harm

why then not me?

One trauma after another

has burgeoned out the blue

surrounding my life in sorrow

what am I to do?

My pain seems unending
peace and happiness is conceptual and abstract
goals and plans for the future
seem atrophied and black.

Every day is a constant struggle
my God what have I done?
how have I offended thee
that you block out all my sun?

Have I done something so bloody wrong
that I am being punished for this way?
Are you a God of vengeance
that makes his children pay?

No, I cannot believe that of my God
for He has been there by my side
always compassionate to my needs
in the many hours that I have cried.

God does not mete out pain
He only delivers love and light
the distress and sorrow that we feel
are all a part of life.

We have chosen a certain path
we may not consciously be aware
selected the avenue that is right for us
despite its dark despair.

Our decision does not create misfortune
life is a tragedy waiting to unfold
but being aware of our greater purpose
is the alchemy that turns lead to gold.

The minutes, hours, and days pass by
like the river that flows to the sea
what was the present moment
again will never be.

So when the woes of tragedy come our way
and death rears its ugly head
one must confront the fact of life
that our loved one is truly dead.

There is no way to bring them back
the facts are as cold as ice
what has happened is the bitter truth
that no rationale can suffice.

Life again will bloom for you
it will not always be this bleak
know in your heart there is a greater good
that has yet to reach its peak.

For those whose paths are filled with hurt
more than their fair share
will gain much more from this life
if they keep their hearts aware.

Happiness will again be yours
a healing will take place
you will recognize your destiny
that you can and will embrace.

It is in recognition of life's kismet
with its portents along the way
that you can find your key to bliss
and find joy in every day.
In the discovery that life has direction

beyond your conscious thought
that divine guidance is always there
whether its cognizant or not.

Destiny is not cast in stone
it can be up or down the hill
the decision with your options
are choices of your free will.

Assess the commonalties in your life
and evaluate the significance that they display
find the direction they point for you
and what they are trying to say.

Follow your bliss as it presents itself
use life's circumstance to grow
become what you are meant to be
surrender and you will know.

Grasp more meaning from your life
give credence to its pain
forge your future, yet manifest
from the knowledge you have gained.

We cannot change what has transpired
but we can modify how we react
knowing that God has a greater purpose
that in us He did enact.

Tragedy will still rise up to meet us
tears will continue to flow from our eyes
but in distinguishing the pattern of synchronicity
you will begin to realize.

To comprehend the greater plan
a personal paradigm of our own
and implement what we have to do
with the seeds that should be sown.

Experience your sorrow as it comes
express the feelings of your grief
know that death is a part of life
that comes in like a thief.

Our bodies are very fragile
life is terminal from the start
and when you lose your loved one
you must know this in your heart.

You are sad, hurt, and lonely
and you have a right to be
but you can choose to grow from this
and fulfill your destiny.

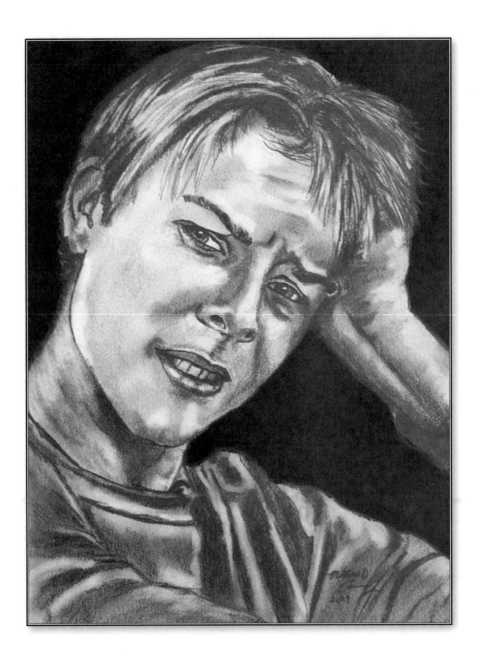

Afterword

WHERE DO WE GO FROM HERE?

Where has all the magic gone
that once had filled my life?
Sacred days...so bittersweet
with my son, my daughter, and my wife.

We fought death with all we had
there was almost nothing we did not try
but despite our every effort
our child still had to die.

We were left in pain and sorrow
but we sought magic through our tears
and found miracles in motion
as we moved on throughout the years.

Those miracles in motion
kept our boat afloat
no dream seemed too bizarre
or a coincidence too remote.

Spontaneous chills and goose bumps
are meant to warm the spirit
they happen when they happen
and happen when you need it.

Years pass and newfound goals
have seemed to slowly fill the space
where once were his deep blue eyes
and the touch of his embrace.

Those days seem so long ago
and so much water has passed under
but I will never forget
all the magic and the wonder.

When God is breathing down your neck
It's because He is holding you real close
You can feel His heartbeat within your own
and find ways that you can cope.

You find a way to transform your grief
into something tangible and good
so light a bonfire in the darkness
let your deeds become the wood.

You must give back to everyone
with everything you can
share your world with others
truly listen, and lend a hand.

You cannot bring a loved one back
there are no rebates from the grave
so one must embrace a living face
and find someone you can save.

Save somebody from their loneliness
save someone from their pain
save them from themselves
or from a society gone insane.

Everyone longs for love
without it we would surely die
it's easy to give in many ways
a smile, a hug…a cry.

So it's "Top-o-the morning" to everyone
let your heart light shine
reach into each other's hearts
with words, with touch…and time.

Makes silly jokes and laugh out loud
it's giggles that massage the soul
look directly into people's eyes
and let your heart light glow.

Others will see that inner light
as you gaze into their eyes
and know we are all relations
the ignorant and the wise.

These words are ruminations
that originate from my heart
and I try to live them daily
for the benefits they impart.

Still there will be difficult times
when sadness escorts travail
nothing tried will ease the pain
and you will feel that you have failed.

This has happened to me
and not that long ago
I wondered where the magic went
and why it had to go.

Where were the miracles that
were once woven within my grief
I used to talk to angels
and had visions in my sleep.

I know that the well never goes dry
God's touch is always there
it's I who have dried my tears
and moved on from my despair.

I can manage by myself, I've said…
others need you by their side
but dear God I miss the magic
that in my life you allowed to reside.

I now realize the miracles never stop
they only take a different form
mini-miracles happen everyday
and soon become the norm.

God's magic has changed my life
changed who and what I am
I have moved through the pain
and find joy in all I can.

Sunrises are crisp again
sunsets bathe my heart
butterflies, birds, and song
are daily works of art.

As the sands of the ocean
were once a piece of land
what once was in human terms
can never be again.

Some flowers bloom for only moments
then wither and fade away
but the memory of their great beauty
is always here to stay.

So we move on with our life
and embrace the miracles that we can find
the magic in essence, never goes away
it's just that sometimes we are blind.

Blind to what is right beside us
or hitting us smack dab in the face
there is no shame in heartfelt empathy
for love it knows no disgrace.

There will be people whom we meet
that we have known for many years
or share moments for the first time
with strangers and their fears.

We must boldly share our love,
reach out to others without hesitation or dismay
find the pain that lies so near
and around us every day.

Whether it's an old friend or an enemy,
a relative or just a cashier at the store
there will be someone who will need you
and it's you who shall open the door.

Be of service to yourself
and with all the people you meet
there are many paths yet to cross
many avenues and streets.

There are people who desperately need
your involvement in their sorrow
just as you need them
to face the next tomorrow.

So if you think that God has overlooked you
and has no idea that you are there
you must realize it's not that He's forgotten
it's you who has forgotten that He's so near.

Miracles and magic are never ever gone
they are always within our reach
just as are the memories of our loved ones
and what they had to teach.

They taught us love is unconditional
it is the strongest fiber in our being
so let loose, let go, let God, let love
let yourself… and start a new beginning.

When one door closes another opens somewhere... be there.

—MC

Great grief is a divine and terrible radiance

which transfigures the wretched.

—Victor Hugo

Prayer for Healers

—Saint Frances of Assisi

Lord make me an instrument of your peace:

where there is hatred, let me sow love;

where there is injury, healing;

where there is doubt, faith;

where there is despair, hope;

where there is darkness, light;

and where there is sadness, joy.

Oh divine Master,

grant that I may not seek

so much to be consoled

as to console;

to be understood as to understand;

to be loved as to love.

For it is in giving that we receive;

it is in healing that we are healed;

and it is in dying that we are born to eternal life.

The Process of Grieving

Stepping at Your Own Pace

The initial intent of this book was to publish my letters to Kelly to help people through the process of their grief. There is no worse pain on this earth than to lose a child, no grief harder to bear. Working on all the material for the publication of this book, I soon realized there was more than just the letters that needed to be shared. The incredible experiences we underwent in those last six months of Kelly's life make a miraculous, unbelievable, and bittersweet tale. Now I will attempt to enlighten you on the gifts that were given to me that were attained only through the experience of losing my son. You can see how Kelly's life and his consummate death touched our lives and the lives of others though this the great ripple effect.

The largest and most obvious obstacle to overcome was Kelly's death—that he just plainly was no longer here with us. It is so hard to accept the unacceptable, the loss of your child, but it is in recognizing the spiritual gifts that you are given in the process of losing a loved one that gives you the strength to move forward. You cannot change the fact of their death but you can modify how you react to it. There is no way to bring them back from the grave, so you have to look at ways of keeping their legacy and memory alive.

You give credence to their life by how you live yours. You can crawl into a hole of self-pity forever, keeping their memory alive in your own selfish ways by your apathy and fear of moving forward. This does nothing for their living memory; it simply makes you a miserable person to be around. Ultimately two lives are wasted. The feelings of deep despair will continue for a long, long time, and you may at times wish for your own death to gain relief. This is okay to feel and a perfectly normal reaction following a devastating loss. You recognize it for what it is, let it in, feel it, and let it go.

I do not believe there are any predictable linear stages in processing the death of a loved one. Although widely accepted for many years, I do not think the five stages of grief, as proposed by Elisabeth Kübler-Ross, adequately represent the reality of the journey for all bereaved. Her groundbreaking stages were derived from her research with people who were dying, not with the bereaved. In their original context the stages are a brilliant theory on the emotional response to dying, which I experienced myself when I was told my son was going to die. I went through denial, anger, bargaining, and depression, just as outlined by Kübler-Ross. But the final stage, acceptance, was accepting the fight; I could *not* accept his death. Processing the reality of your own death and finding acceptance is one thing, but accepting that your child is going to die is another.

In the downstream processing of my own loss after Kelly's death, I soon found the stages did not apply in theory or in their outlined order to the events of my grief journey. I felt frustrated, as did many other bereaved parents I had met. Because Kübler-Ross's stages have become so ubiquitous, we all knew of them, so we felt that we weren't grieving properly or passing through the stages in the right order. I have since come to learn that Kübler-Ross herself stated before her death in 2004, "There is not a typical response to loss, as there is no typical loss. Our grieving is as individual as our lives."

I believe the journey is more like a series of steps negotiated one at a time, each one taking as long as it takes to reach the next—no timetable, no shortcuts, no false expectations, no failures, just one step at a time, climbing the "stairs" when we are ready, willing, and able. Each person's stairway has the same steps, but they are processed uniquely and different for everyone. Whether it is a long-term illness that took our loved one's life, a sudden unexpected accident, murder, or suicide, it is we who are left behind who will have to climb this stairway.

S.T.A.I.R.S.
The Six Steps in Surviving Loss

The first step is <u>S</u>hock. Our loved one dies; we are in reactionary disbelief, and we are numb head to *soul*. This is how we are able to choose a casket, sign papers, read sympathy cards, and publicly share our grief with so many. We are in a primal stage of survival; we function as an automaton and accomplish the impossible: we bury or cremate the body of our loved one.

The second step is <u>T</u>rauma. This is the ensuing reality of our loss and our struggle to comprehend it and weave it into the fabric that is our daily lives. This may be the step where the bereaved linger the longest. This is when we go through the motions of daily life while constantly struggling to cope with our loss. We return to work; we participate in holidays; but every morning we open our eyes after our fitful night's sleep to again sword fight with denial and disbelief. The light of each new day beckons us to rejoin the world that we are reticent to embrace. To move forward, to function at all in the everyday world, gives us the feeling that we are dishonoring our loved one. We know there is no going back, but we do not want to move forward. So we stay where we are for as long as it takes.

The third step is **<u>A</u>cceptance/Absorption**. This is the most powerful step in processing our loss, when we accept the loss has taken place and absorb the ramifications it has on our lives. We begin to make plans for the future, as nebulous as it may seem. This is not an easy admission to make but a crucial one for our survival. Accepting the reality of the loss is not forgetting or letting go of our loved one; it's living with the loss and accepting its collateral damage to our future.

The fourth step is **<u>I</u>ntrospection/Insight**. This is where we look deep within ourselves to try and find ourselves. We question our faith and seek to find the "meaning of life" in the depths of our sorrow. We use the tools of intuition, gut feelings, and prayer to access the world, inside and out, in a different light of perception. The more we know, the more we know what we don't know. We look to find answers to the whys and the cries of our wounded souls…and we are finally willing to hear the answers.

The fifth step is **<u>R</u>einvestment/Rebuilding**. This is where we take charge of our journey and find creative and healthy ways to process our loss. This is what I call *proactive grieving*, when we earnestly attempt to reconstruct the foundation of a life that has been shattered and try to regain the joy that is our birthright. We become *intentional survivors*. This is when we can make a difference in the world and fulfill our personal destiny. When we honor our loved one's life by creating a legacy in their name, the world is enriched instead of diminished.

The sixth step is **<u>S</u>erenity** and true peace. This is not always possible in this world, whether you have experienced loss or not, but it is attainable. Serenity may take years or even decades to reach, or it may creep into our lives on the journey itself…when we are caught by surprise at seeing a smiling face in the mirror. Miracles do happen…believe.

Grief is complex and unyielding, and if not dealt with in some pro-active manner, it can lead to post–traumatic stress disorder years down the road. Active participation in our grief journey is paramount to healthy survival. If we want to feel good again, feel joy again, feel part of the world again, we should strive to become intentional survivors and not a hapless victims. Seek help; read; journal; reach out to others in pain; set a goal, no matter how small; grieve outside of the box; mourn; and lament without shame. Live your loss; ascend those stairs know-ing that you must do so to survive. It will not be easy and may take a long time to move from step to step. Time itself becomes a stranger; we are looking through a different lens, feeling stuck between the outside world and the reality of our world. With no horizon in sight, we wait to see what the next day brings with apathy and resignation. Please real-ize that gravity increases dramatically during the grieving process... so take it slow baby steps, one at a time.

Grief contains a variety of emotions that come as they may. There is no emotional map to follow or chart that will reveal your individual path. Emotions surface when you least expect. When it happens, do not be embarrassed or cover them up. Instead, experience them; good friends who understand will give you a hug or give you your space. There is no one way to grieve, only your way. Grief is hard work, and there is no way around it, only thorough it—and it takes as long as it takes.

Turning Loss into Legacy

There are greater things in store for you in this life, many things to accomplish, and many lives to touch. Strive to look at your situation as an opportunity for your own personal growth. In growing from our losses, we in essence keep our loved ones' legacies alive by the positive actions we choose in our daily lives. You substantiate their life by the way you live yours. This not only benefits others by your interaction with their lives but also keeps the memory of your loved one alive and ever present in your heart and in the world at large.

I love my life more than ever before. I believe that Kelly has survived death. I believe his living and vibrant energy is with me every second of every day; we are partners across the veil. My life and the lives of my family have been changed forever in so many positive ways. Kelly's death has propelled me into a world of caring, compassion, and love. I look at life as what can I do for others—how can I help to heal the pain of others and make the world a better place.

Providing assistance for people in grief, despair, and the pangs of death not only helps others but it can also help in every aspect of your life. When we were living in California, I went to massage school to be able to massage Kelly and ease some of his discomfort. Since that time, I have provided massage for many terminally ill and grieving people. Joining the AIDS massage project (AMP) has helped dozens of people with the pains of their disease and the process of their dying. I have facilitated grief groups and have helped others to cope with the loss of a loved one, paying special attention to parents whom have lost a child. I have helped them prepare for the passing over of their child, assisting with making the funeral plans, and helping to rebuild their lives for months and sometimes years following their losses. By helping others, I have expanded my world, my heart, and my love; through my actions, Kelly's legacy thrives.

Aiding the grieving and dying is only one of many possible forms of legacy you can engage in. For the past twenty-five years, I have given blood on a monthly basis, totaling over 35 gallons of blood donated which has helped to save or extend the life of over five hundred individuals. Being involved with the Red Cross, I have organized blood drives, and more recently, bone marrow testing drives to recruit more volunteers for the National Bone Marrow Donor database. Although I've been on the database for twenty years, I have never been called for a potential match, but it is on record and available, the potential is there. My daughter Meagan was tested at one of the drives and was just recently found to be a match for a patient. At the time of this writing, she is in round two of testing and waiting for more test results. This is another way one can participate in a miracle and literally help save someone's life. This form of giving is incredibly valuable, as it saves or extends the lives of hundreds each year with such a small personal sacrifice.

This is what I have done and what has worked for me, but I believe anyone who becomes more centered in their altruistic nature and begins giving to others will soon discover it becomes a lifestyle. You will find yourself opening more doors for people (physically and metaphorically), becoming a better automobile driver, a better tipper, a better citizen, and ultimately a better person. This becomes addicting, for when you give, you get so much back, and life again becomes a joy. These are the gifts my son has given me. The best part of this process is that, through your good works, you can affect change in other people. Once you have instilled a positive change in a person, they may go on to change others, and so on and so on in a progressive ripple effect.

Energy does not dissipate; it only changes form and moves ever onward. Everyone has to face the fact they will ultimately lose someone they love some time in their life. We should not have to wait until we lose that person to share our love with others in a positive way that can help heal people and the planet as a whole. Love is that embodiment of intelligent design that most people personify as God. Strive to love God with all your heart; believe in miracles and in the magic of life. Have faith in your ability to survive your loss.

Twenty-three years later, I still marvel at all that happened to us through the experiences of our son's life and his death. Over ten years ago, following a corporate merger, I lost my job of some twenty odd years. I was responsible for safety, a position I had held for three years and took very seriously. In that time the injury rates dropped dramatically, so much, in fact, we received a national award. Wherever you are, with the right action and intention , you can affect positive change or plant seeds of change.

Losing a job is a devastating reality. We had just recently purchased a five-acre hobby farm in the country. We were supporting four horses, cats, dogs, and a whole litany of other animals and activities. My daughter was soon to graduate from high school and would be starting college. My wife works as a Registered Nurse in ICU at a local hospital. She was making an adequate income, but I needed a job to literally save the farm. My experiences involving Kelly's loss have made trusting my gut feelings an intrinsic part of my daily life, so I put my faith in God.

After the loss of my job, there were a few rough months, but I let go and left it in the hands of God. Soon I found myself working at St. Elizabeth Ann Seton School, a small K-8 parochial school not fifteen minutes from the farm. I had retained my boilers' license from my previous position and used it to land the job as the boiler engineer/maintenance man at this little school. I love it at the school. Seeing four hundred kids everyday is a continual joy to me. In my memories, my son will always physically be a nine-year-old boy. When I see all the boys at school and watch them grow through the years, I can imagine my son growing with them. This is truly a gift.

I have become an active part of the children's life in school. They recognize me as an artist, so in the early hours before school, I put gold stars on all my favorite artwork in the hallways. The kids now anticipate getting a star on their artwork and are doing excellent work to get one. Being a Catholic school, the atmosphere is a very joy-filled one, with emphasis on spirit. There is singing all the time, which continually lifts the spirit and nourishes the soul. I also have become involved with the kids in their singing. I have taught students how to use sign language with several songs they sing at Mass. I intend to start a signing choir in the very near future. The kids love me and I them. It is the best job

I have ever had. I feel better physically, mentally, emotionally, and am charged with the exhilaration of knowing I am on the right path. It is life changing and miraculous.

Change is the only constant we have in life. In adapting to that change and using it as an opportunity for growth and benevolence, you will begin to see the pattern that was meant for your life. As opposed to the twelve- to fourteen-hour days that I had spent at the refinery, at the school, I now work a standard eight-hour day. The pay is a whole lot less, but you adjust your lifestyle accordingly. I lost some income, but have gained so much more—the adage "less is more" has now become very real. This change has afforded me the time to work on my gardens, ride my horse, see more sunsets on my deck, visit with friends, pursue my altruistic endeavors, work on my artwork, and, of course, finish my book. I made a promise to myself and to my son that I would write our story, publish it, and share it with the world. This I have done. Life is good. In embracing the legacy of your loved one's loss, your life can be too.

> *Do or do not; there is no try."*
>
> —Yoda

Whispers of Love

Since this book's first publication, I have spoken to thousands of bereaved individuals who have experienced phenomenon that support the notion that spirit survives physical death. I call these experiences "whispers of love."

If you have lost someone close to you and suffer with that loss, you may have wished for, prayed for, expected, and/or anticipated some sort of supernatural experience that would validate your belief that there truly is life after death. I believe that, somehow, our loved ones who have moved on in spirit can communicate to us in some form or fashion and that it can bring us a peace that can be found no other way. I believe we live in one sphere of existence while our departed loved ones live in another, but we can meet at the seam where our worlds connect. If our love is strong, and we keep all our senses open, it can and will happen. All we need is to let go of fear of the unknown and our own preconceived notions of what and what is not real.

Recently I have become a grandfather again and cannot believe the depth of love that I have for these children. At this point in my life, on a bereavement journey of almost twenty years, I had thought I had hit a plateau of acceptance with the death and physical loss of my son Kelly. I had accepted that my heart would never quite feel the intensity of joy that it once had. My grandchildren have brought that level of joy back to my heart that I thought was gone forever. With that joy has come some unexpected blessings—some very special visits from our son.

I think Kelly stuck his foot in the door when his niece, baby Kinsey, came to this world. When she was about six months old I was holding her and rocking her in my arms while Meagan was packing the car, and she fell sound asleep. I carefully put her in the car seat and strapped her in. While I doing so her eyes blinked open staring right into mine, and I audibly gasped as I was staring into the eyes of my son. Kelly was looking back at me just as surely as I was breathing. Her eyes closed again, joining her body in deep slumber. I could not help myself and whispered "Is that you, Kelly?" Her eyes immediately snapped open again and she smiled a broad smile for a second and fell back sound asleep. I believe he is lingering close to us for awhile; it has been quite a long time since we felt his energy this profoundly. There were many years of silence (or possibly there was too much white noise of life in the way for us to hear), but we feel so blessed that he continues to surprise us with his visits and everlasting love.

Many, many people have had some form of experience with communication from a loved one who has died. Most people are afraid to tell others, fearing that they will be considered "nuts," having gone off the deep end or lost it completely, desperate for anything to assuage their pain. For the most part, I believe people are afraid of what they don't understand. Just using the word "ghost" conjures up thoughts of scary things, so we use words more palatable to our psyche, such as "presence," "spirit," "angel," "visitation," "entity," "soul," or "energy field"—verbiage that takes away the enigma of darkness that surrounds communication from spirit world. People are frightened of the unknown and attribute signs or spectral visits to some malevolent spirit instead of merely whispers of love from our deceased loved ones.

Communications from beyond the grave bring to mind nineteenth-century séances with unsettled spirits raising tables and blowing out candles. The modern image of this phenomenon is eerie, creepy, and fraught with charlatans that prey on the vulnerable and the bereaved. Twentieth-century Hollywood brought us many movies filled with ghosts, specters, and poltergeists who continue to perpetuate the belief in evil spirits who have a want and need to frighten us. Spirit communications have been mystified and sensationalized for so long it has become ingrained in our collective psyche as a negative experience when it is merely love trying to shine through the veil of darkness.

Some religions have also helped to perpetuate the urban legends of entities that are bent on plaguing humankind. Many religious leaders teach that trying to connect with discarnate spirits (with an Ouija board or a medium, for example) is dangerous, that the methods used are based on arcane or evil practices and one is investing in the dark side by participating in it. Yet most religions are based on prophets who hear voices, have spoken with angels, and have communicated with people long dead. The concept of speaking with the dead goes back to ancient times and is not going away anytime soon because it happens every day. We just need to demystify it.

Orbs in photos, lights turning on and off, hearing voices, things being misplaced, a cool breeze from nowhere, doors slamming, phones ringing, dogs barking at nothing, and on and on. Most people historically attribute these "happenings" to evil spirits or poltergeists. They believe the life energies of the departed are somehow stuck on earth and unable to join our creator, that they cling to the earth to haunt and to scare those left behind. I prefer to believe these happenings are our loved ones using what is available to let us know they are around us always.

Love is the light of the world, the energy that keeps the balance within us and the universe at large. Attaining balance is the yin and the yang of cosmic consciousness that opens the door to spirit. I do not believe disembodied spirits could make themselves known to us without love, but with love they are empowered to do so. Our love empowers us to receive it. They use whatever they can and whatever is available to get our attention to say, "Hello! It's me, pay attention!" So things go bump in the night; lights go on and off. Society labels it as a poltergeist or some evil phantom when it is only our loved ones trying to get our attention and letting us know that their love lives on.

The spirits of our loved ones can even enter our dreams and speak to us in such a way that cannot be dismissed as "just a dream." A dream visitation is usually in full color, like watching a movie, and leaves a powerful impression; you can remember it years later as vividly as the day it happened. During the dream you can experience smells and emotions, taste the tears, feel the pain and the love. Your mind, body, and spirit react to it as is if it was real; you remember the experience as it if was real. You do so because it was not "just a dream;" it *was* real. When we have an after-death communication experience, our bodies react accordingly; endorphins are released that can actually help relieve physical and emotional pain.

Sighing and moaning does the same thing. Both send gentle vibrations softly throughout the body, triggering the release of endorphins and lessening pain. Deep moaning, as from a physical trauma, or intense screams, as from child birth, are the body's attempt to alleviate pain. Crying and laughing are flip sides of the same coin and also trigger this same release of endorphins. So sigh away, cry away, and allow the laughter; it does help ease the pain. Embrace the love; embrace the light. With the light comes healing. Our loved ones are with us always, so filter out the white noise of life and speak to them from your heart and in prayer. Listen closely with all your senses, for love cannot be denied. It was and is always there... and only a whisper away.

Sing as if no one were listening, dance as if no one were watching...

And live everyday as if it were your last.

—Old Irish Proverb

Collateral Blessings

We can suffer collateral losses downstream from the loss of our loved one which can extend and complicate the journey. Paradoxically we can also be gifted with collateral blessings. I want to share several stories I believe illustrate the healing power of synchronicity, serendipity, and the power of prayer—where magic and faith combines.

Saint Gilbert of Ensenada

On December 1, 1987, life as our family knew it ceased to exist. I watched helplessly as my nine-year-old son's tired and cancer-ravaged body slowly released his spirit. I saw his partially paralyzed face find its proper form, and like the graceful arch of a feather, his smile returned once more. His half-slit eyes, almost crusted closed, yawned wide open, and the dark slate of his irises returned to brilliant blue, like forget-me-nots floating in a pool of cream. In the split seconds of my half gasp, the soft glow went out, and blue faded again back to gray. Although I knew I had just looked in to the eyes of God, I crumbled to the floor and wept.

Something shifted within my soul that day that has never shifted back. I became a different me; a survivor emerged with no key to the future. One door closed, but a new one did not swing open. I had no key, no clue to my future; only the closed doors of uncertainty and nebulous refuge stood in front of me. My tomorrow had been stolen from me, and like a new born baby, I cried to be held and rocked, hoping sleep would come forever.

At day's next dawning, when I first awoke, denial appeared and "it all must have been a dream" screamed loudly from my soul. Cruel daylight brought back the shades of gray in my shadow lands, and reality threw its cold water on my face. I was brought quickly back to the harsh reality of life; I knew it was not an awful dream. My son had died; his lifeless body was no longer on the couch, no death watch today... only the gray. Everything sounded so quiet or muffled to my ears, so much seemed strangely unfamiliar. I felt like a stranger in my own dream in a house not my own. How could this have happened? How could I possibly live without my son?

Many of us in this life will be faced with these same questions that have no answers, and we struggle to survive. How we survive is different for each of us. Not surviving sounds like an attractive option, but not a rational one. Like a newborn baby, we are thrust into a new world, one we have to learn to live in all over again.

As a bereaved parent, I am now twenty-three years old in grief years, and it is time to tell you a little more of the ensuing journey that has, this many years later, brought me much peace. After my son died following a two-year battle with cancer, I fell into an abyss of despair. We had fought for so long to save his life with everything in our power. We had great physicians, surgeons, oncologists, a great children's hospital, and great insurance, but they were not enough. They still could not save our son from his ultimate death to cancer. We took it a step beyond, a step in faith to heal our son.

The publishing of this book and making my grief three-dimensional was a huge milestone in processing my grief and subsequently a spring board to a future I had never conceived of or envisioned. We had remortgaged our house to publish the book of my son's life, his death, his healing, our miracle, our journey. It was a book mainstream publishers would not touch, so I self-published and transformed the most intimate details of a family's worst tragedy into an inspirational source of healing for the bereaved.

As you may recall from earlier in the book, the Make-A-Wish Foundation agreed to send us to Hawaii for two weeks. We were then to return home for more palliative radiation. On our return from the Islands and with the advice of my nephew, we traveled to Mexico for a day to locate some healing herbs to help our son's recovery from the assaults of chemotherapy. We ended up staying for two months, and Kelly experienced the miracle healing.

Manieadera, you may recall, is small fishing village just south of Ensenada near the famous landmark La Bufadora which is a natural seawater blowhole on the Pacific side of the Baja (one of three in the world). It has now become a popular cruise ship tourist stop.

Meagan was only six years old when we lived in Mexico, and through the years I have always told her that, when the time was right, we would return to Ensenada, back to that little fishing village and the little chapel where the miracle occurred so long ago. Boyfriends came and went, but the significant other in her life that would warrant the journey (that felt right), never appeared in her life until just a few years ago. She fell in love with a wonderful young man, the real deal, a genuine man with tenderness and depth of character. They had a child together, our grandchild and a new light in all of our lives. At last we felt like the time was right to make our pilgrimage back to Mexico. We started to make plans.

To drive to Ensenada you have to drive through Tijuana and navigate the long coastal road for several hours. Maniedera would be an hour beyond Ensenada, if we could even find it after so many years.

Driving your own car or a rental both are considered risky with the current instances of *banditos* accosting tourists who attempt to make the drive. We saw an ad for a cruise ship that sailed to Ensenada and booked it for the four of us for an October cruise that would at least bring us to Ensenada.

Before we left Minnesota, I envisioned what I wanted to happen once we were in Ensenada. I prayed that we would just get off the boat, walk up to a trustworthy, English-speaking taxi cab driver, and I would offer him a hundred bucks for four hours to take us to La Bufadora and on the way there see if he could help us find the little chapel near Manieadera. I carefully tucked a crisp new one hundred dollar bill into the back of my wallet just for this purpose.

While on board the ship, we asked about hiring a driver once we arrived in Ensenada. They did not recommend doing any touring that was not offered through their itinerary and discouraged us from doing so. If we wanted to pursue it on our own, we were free to do so, but they were not responsible for our safety. On top of that, we would have to make the twenty-minute walk into town to inquire.

We got off the boat prepared to walk into the center of town. We passed the many Carnival Cruise Line posted tour buses that people were cuing for to take the hour or so drive to see the famous La Bufadora. We only had about a five-hour window to find our chapel, so we started to walk quickly. Just past the last of the big tour buses sat a lonely white van with a small sign in the window, which simply stated: "Shuttle Service For Hire." It appeared to be a brand new van, despite the very faded "Tips Accepted" sign (which was the reverse side of the sign). I had walked by the van at first and then retraced my steps to see if there was a driver inside. He got out of his van and asked me if I was looking to hire a taxi.

I said we were, that we wanted to go to La Bufadora but also do several hours of more personal sightseeing on the way. He smiled broadly and, with a knowing wink in his eye, said in perfect English, "How about four hours for a hundred bucks?" I about fell over but calmly said that would be fine.

He brought out a little step stool to help us into the van, shut the double doors, sat back in the driver's seat and announced, "Hi, my name is Gilbert. Where to first?"

I explained that, although we did want to travel to La Bufadora (as it is well worth the visit and was a part of our nostalgic tour) we really wanted to find the village of Maniadera above all else. Did he know of the village? He responded that, although he was from Ensenada, he had gone to school in Maniadera and knew how to get there. We talked more, and I told him a little of our experience of twenty-one years ago and why we wanted to find the chapel and to possibly find and walk on the beach where we had lived so long ago. He said much had changed over the years. Maniadera had spread out in all directions, but he thought he could get us near the beach area that we hoped to see.

On the drive I told him about the miracle healing that we had experienced and the genteel older woman who owned the chapel. I mentioned her name was Doña Nieves but that she was also known as Señora Fisher. His eyes lit up immediately. "I went to school with her son. I know where her house is and even possibly the chapel of which you speak. I heard she died about eight years ago, but her son may live there now. I am certain we can find it."

Soon the smells and geography started to take on a familiar quality, like glimpses of a recurring dream teasing at your body, mind, and soul. The olfactory senses are the strongest trigger that can retrieve the deepest of memories, even those gained as a child, and my daughter was experiencing it big time. Every place on earth seems to have its own smell and flavor. Fishing docks, dead seaweed, ocean breeze, hints of raw sewage and blooming cacti brought us back to those long-forgotten days almost immediately.

In my daughter's hands, she clutched an old shirt her brother had last worn when we lived here. She had surprised us by packing it in her purse for this purpose, if and when we found the chapel. A few wrong turns and a closed road later, we found ourselves parked in front of the chapel that had changed our life so many years before. We all got out of the van, still stunned that we had found it at all.

The same flower patterned curtains still hung in the tiny windows on either side of the chapel door, and the simple wooden cross still adorned the peak of the modest roofline—it still looked the same. Soon a woman came out of the main house, and I was sure she was wondering why these four American tourists were standing so reverently and speechless in front her husband's machine shed. Saint Gilbert came to the rescue again. Through his interpretation, he explained the story and why we were there.

The kind lady was the daughter-in-law of the late Señora Fisher, and she confirmed that the old woman had died. She also said that, although the building was now her husband's machine shed, it was indeed the little chapel that Señora Fisher had built for healing. We could not go inside, but we were allowed to take some photos in front of the chapel. When through, we graciously thanked her and left.

We took a short walk to the beach and soon lost ourselves in quiet gratefulness, savoring so many memories that were flooding our beings. We looked for the beach house where he had lived those few magical months. We knew from relatives that the house, itself, had burned to the ground less than a year after we had stayed there and had been built over again. It was difficult to ascertain where the exact spot was, but it made no difference. We were there. We felt it.

We then took a very quiet ride to La Bufadora and ate some delicious fish and shrimp tacos, sipped bottles of cold Corona beer and pondered our miracle as it was happening. Our angel, our friend, Saint Gilbert of Ensenada had certainly come through. We walked back to our van after our light repast and asked Gilbert to take us back to the town of Ensenada to seek memories yet to be revealed.

On the drive back, I told Gilbert we used to frequent a place back when we were here last. It was only a street vendor, but they had the best tacos I have ever had in my life. The stall used to be on the corner of Seis and Ruiz in a non-tourist part of town. Gilbert exclaimed with excitement, "I was just there yesterday! How do you know of the best kept secret of Ensenada?" He took us right there. Nothing, I mean absolutely nothing, had changed at all. My God, it looked like the same place I had walked up to twenty-one years prior, and we had the best tasting treat of a lifetime. El Norteno was still open for business.

The store front was just a cubby hole with a green and white tiled counter housing the cook, the grill, a white chest refrigerator, a soda cooler, and the lady cashier. You ordered how many you wanted, and when you were full you gave her the count of how many eaten and paid up. It had not changed one iota in twenty-one years. There just happened to be a local musician leaning against his pickup serenading all who were ordering and those who were eating. No place to sit, you stand and enjoy. The first bite of that little taco gave me a vivid jolt of another place, another time. It seems the physical sense of taste now ameliorated with the other five senses, and for a brief moment I was totally back to a life lived so long ago. I was swept away.

Paying for our nine tacos, one torta, and two Coke lights, we left to find Gilbert waiting silently in the alley. I pulled that crisp one hundred dollar bill from my wallet, along with a few hundred pesos that we had left to give as a tip. I almost had to push it in his hands, as he seemed reluctant and embarrassed to even take it. We hugged warmly as I placed it in his hands, cupping them tightly, and simply said, "Thank you, Gilbert. Thank you so very much."

He modestly responded, "Good memories I am sure you had, as well as some sad ones. Via con Dios my friends…" He nodded his head with that same knowing wink he gave me four hours earlier on the pier. He then disappeared from our lives as quickly as he had entered it. We were touched by an angel, Saint Gilbert of Ensenada.

We returned home to a chilly Minnesota October with our bodies tanned, spirits filled, and still somewhat in awe of the journey we had just taken. I walked the gardens around the farm, which had obviously experienced a hard frost in our absence. Most of the leaves on the plants and flowers were a dark, cucumber green and drooping, loosely attached to the still-yielding firm stems. Soon I was surprised to find a batch of forget-me-nots seemingly unscathed from Jack Frost's touch. They stood defiant amongst the other browning flora and scattered leaves.

These flowers had been planted as seedlings in the spring. They had thrived, but although they are a spring-blooming plant, they did not bloom in the spring or in the summer, not at all…until our return from Ensenada. In the center of the patch was one tall stem with the most brilliant tiny blue flowers I have ever seen. Seeing them was like staring into my son's eyes. I felt warm all over with an indescribable blast of God tingles, and I heard Kelly clearly say to me, "You have not forgotten me; I will forget you not."

The Jim Trudeau Story

In early 1986 my son Kelly was very sick from battling cancer, and a police officer named Jim Trudeau came to our house out of the blue to see our son. This Washington County deputy sheriff pulled out his wallet and took from it his sheriff's badge and pinned on my son's frail chest. He then deputized Kelly a "special honorary sheriff." That was the only time we had ever met this man, but I have never forgotten him.

Almost 20 years later, my wife recognized this sheriff as a patient in the hospital where she works. When she told me that she had seen him, I was overjoyed to know his whereabouts. I had always wanted to thank him for that very important small act of kindness so long ago.

Although Kelly wore the badge the officer had given him in his casket, we had kept it from cremation, and it soon became an almost forgotten keepsake in my wife's jewelry chest. Years later I felt a deep tugging inside me that it was important to give it back to the sheriff. I dug it out of the jewelry box, pinned it on the cover of my book, and sent it to him in a package, thanking him for his selfless act of kindness so long ago. Little did we know how important this gesture was going to be for him … until I received this letter from Jim in January of 2005. With his permission I share it with you now.

January 11, 2005
Dear Barb and Mitch,

For some time, I have wanted to write this letter/story, I really don't know which it is—maybe a journey? First of all in my humble opinion "Kelly James" is still keeping busy, if there is such a thing as a guardian angel— he's mine. When I came to your house in Bayport in 1986 to see Kelly, we talked about him meeting God before me and that he should take care of him (God) until I got there and then we would work together as a team or partners. But I'm not sure he ever left my side, he certainly never left my thoughts and I used his bravery as an example so many times when teaching at police training classes or as an inspiration to folks during hard times.

Allow me to fast forward to my retirement party in July, 1994 after twenty-nine years in law enforcement. It was a great night, with my loving wife at my side. After several awards, it was my time to give my retirement speech. Earlier that night someone in the crowd of almost three hundred people had asked what was the most special or meaningful thing I had done in all my years of police work. I responded by saying "that's in my farewell speech."

When Carol and I stepped to the podium, I reminisced about getting a good friend to the hospital in time before he went into cardiac arrest and the time a deputy and I pulled a six-year-old from the lake, giving him mouth-to-mouth and reviving him. But the most very special meaningful thing in my heart was the time I spent with a little boy in Bayport, Minnesota. His name was Kelly Carmody.

I told them of Kelly's battle and how brave he was and what an inspiration he was to me in my career. Although many tears were shed, several people approached me to say what a heartwarming and inspiring story it was. So in keeping with my normal whirlwind lifestyle, three days later I started my next career as the Executive Director of the Minnesota Sheriffs' Association. One of the many parts of the job was training and you guessed it, young Mr. Carmody just happened to slip into many of my presentations. My story was simple, a reminder of just how lucky we in law enforcement are. "We face danger often, see lots of pain and agony, see people at their worst, face intense stress and pressure in the profession, but we are still lucky that we have lived as long as we have and been given the opportunity to serve. You see, my friend Kelly never got that chance. He never had a girlfriend, got married, drove a car, or had kids. Be happy with the one big gift you have, the gift of life."

After seven years at the Sheriffs' Association and a few health problems— seven angioplasties, eight angiograms, congestive heart failure, and several other maladies, my doctor at Mayo Clinic suggested I retire, which I did in the spring of 2002, even though I loved my job. Carol and I had moved to Inver Grove Heights when I changed jobs in 1994. I really wanted to move back home to Forest Lake, partly because that was home to me but also because of a well-kept secret, I had begun to pass blood and was really afraid to tell anyone.

If it wasn't for Carol insisting I seek medical help, I probably wouldn't be writing this letter/story today. After the much feared and dreaded colonoscopy, Dr. B- told me an operation was my only choice. Although the surgery was traumatic and painful, the worst and totally unexpected result was the reaction to the narcotics and pain medications. Every time I would sleep, I would get horrible flashbacks of murder, suicides, car accidents, drownings, autopsies, and reliving getting shot at the scene of a burglary in 1974. I guess that's when Barb comes into the picture, she apparently told you, Mitch, about me being in the hospital and the trouble I was having. I don't think I could ever find a way to describe the emotional pain I was experiencing. If it wasn't for Carol, I am not sure I could have made it.

Then it happened. The mail came on the morning of January 11, 2003. When your book slid out of the envelope and I saw Kelly and then the badge, my life started again. After I read your letters, I broke down and cried in Carol's arms. For you see, until that time, I didn't care if I lived another day. Even with the strong love and support from Carol who seldom left my side. But there was my little blue-eyed friend looking me right in the eye, how could I give up, he never did. Your letters, your book, the badge, and Kelly got me going again. After reading Letters to My Son *Carol ordered copies for our kids and other family members.*

About two weeks later, I gave the opening address to the newly-elected sheriffs from the 2002 elections. In my presentation, I told them of almost giving up three weeks earlier and what happened when I receive my Carmody care package. All forty-two sheriffs gave me a standing ovation for over five minutes. Each one stood in line and shook my hand, each commenting on the Kelly Carmody story.

After that, I decided as soon as I could go one week without telling my/our Kelly story, that I would then write you this letter/story. I finally gave up, Carol and I left for Venice, Florida on January 4, 2005. But not before I shared Kelly's story with a friend at our local coffee shop on January 3. So why write to you today, January 11? Because it has been two years today since you, Kelly, and Carol have helped me get better. Every once in a while I open your book (it's in the top drawer of my night stand), read your letters, look at that badge, look at Kelly, and think we aren't done yet, are we?! By the way, your book also made the trip to Florida with us and sits on the night stand here by my bed.

Thank you both.

Love,
Jim Trudeau

P.S. If it's okay with you, my Guardian Angel and I still have work to do!

Letter from Lasha…a Whisper of Love

In my work with the bereaved over the past twenty years, I have heard thousands upon thousands of stories that support the belief that there is life after death on some level, on some sphere of existence that is inexplicable and profound. There is simply no other explanation for the common experiences of so many bereaved.

Of the best examples of this phenomenon is in a hand-written letter I received after the first edition was published in 2003. I have received hundreds of personal correspondences from people who have experienced some form of communication from a deceased love one, but this one stands out. It says so much, so beautifully, so honestly. It gives such a vivid portrait of an account with a loved one whom has died and is a quintessential example of consciousness surviving death.

This very powerful *whisper of love* story was sent to me from a young Native American mom who lost her young daughter in an auto accident. Her daughter was killed while she remained in a coma for a time. During her coma she visited with her daughter. This is her unedited story just as I had received it. While it is painful to read the horror of her experience, it brings with it a peace that is beyond moving.

①   9-14-03

       Hello, my name is Lasha Tilsen. I was given your book "Letters to my son" as a gift. To show me others who have lost a loved Child of theres. I would like to share my story.

       It was March 14, 2001, I gave brith to a eye Catching little girl. Her name became Mika. She grow up so fast. She did everything possible in her early days. She started walking at 9 months. She spoke three languages, Spanish, English, Sign, all at around four months of age. She started using the bathroom at one years old. She also Started holding her breath and going under water to swim at 13 months. She did as much as she could get out of Life.

       Now its June of 2002, Mika and I (her mother) went to Porcupine, South Dakota for my Cousin's year momorial of his death. We stayed on the Reservation with othe family members who live there. Mika loved it here, She was home. Her face glowed, her eyes lite up, She found her touch with the spirit word. This reservation was where Wounded Knee was located.

       It was the day before my cousin Eli's momorial and everyone was getting everything together. The whole day was busy and fun. Mika played with

②

other children. She had a great day.
It was after noon and we had to
drive to get things for tomorrow.
One of the trips we drove by Wounded
Knee. As we drove by Mika started screaming.
She looked out the window and screamed.
When she put her head down she was
fine. She started playing a game just
to see if what see was seeing was real.
Bring her head up to see out the   n
window and bring it down. It was like
see could see what happened during
Wounded Knee. The second we drove
out of Wounded Knee her eye lite up
and a smile went across her cheeks.
      Later that night we had another
run to do. It was around 8:00 pm.
It was Mika's bed time but she wanted
to come. I put her in the car seat.
My cousin was driving and her friend
in the passenger seat. I sat in back
with my daughter. Not even one minute
after leaving Mika started screaming.
I knew she was tierd. She usually
nurses to go to bed. I asked my cousin
if I can nurse her. (mika) My cousin
said sure. I unbackted myself and
took my daughter out of the car seat.
Right at the second we were in Wounded
Knee and The Accident happened.

③

My Cousin lost controll of the car. The roads are also very bad at the reservation. The Car went off the road and flipped 3 times on the Side and 3 times on the front. I held on to Mika so she wouldn't get hurt. Mika and myself flow 98 feet from the car. I held onto my daughter intell I hit a brabwire fence. I let go after I went through the fence.

Laying on the ground I was looking at Mika. She was looking at me as well. My Uncle and othe Cousin drove up and ran to us. The two in the car had minor injurys. The Cousin who was with my Uncle ran to me and tied me up with sheets to help the bleeding. The was one cop car there. My Uncle grabbed Mika and took her in the cop car. They went to a Hospital. When I saw my daughter leave. I screamed and tryed leave my body to get to you. My cousin brought me back 3 times. It took 45 minutes for an ambulence to get there.

My eyes where shut but I was still alive. I was in a coma for eight days. The Coma helped me be here today. As I was in the Coma I talked to my daughter mika.

④

We were on the reservation playing on a stream with turtles. She looked at me and said "Mom, what are you doing here?" "I'm here with you." I said. Mika said "No, go back." "I cant go back, I need to stay with you." I said. "It's not your time mom, its my time to be here. I will be alright I will be with them." Mika said pointing behind her. Behind her was a foggy white/gray hall. There I say my great grandmother and my grandma. Then Mika said "You need to go back to your body and let the ones who love you take care of you and you need to take care of all the children and people you love."

I remembering waking up after that. In sign I asked were Mika was. My mother told me what happened. I wasent shocked because I knew she was safe. The doctors almost had to amputate one of my legs when I was in a coma. My mother told them not intell I wake up and they tell me. By the time I woke up my pulse was back. I've had brain surgeries and reconstructive surgeries and others. A totall of seventeen surgeries. I am now talking, walking and knowing my reason for still being alive.

⑤

I believe in God, I believe God sent my daughter to me as my spirit guide. She did what she was her for, now she's still my spirit guide but as she watches over me. I also believe everyone has a reason for being alive. My daugter told me what I need to do. My Theropies are done 10/2003, then I can do what I need to in life.

I have healed in more ways then Just seeing doctors. (medical ones) I've been to Sun dance, Sweats and both brought me to God and the Spirit world. They also have been able to get pain from me that other doctors cant releave.

Thank you for letting me share my story to you. I Know without my conversation with my daughter I wouldnt be as strong or doing so well.

yours truely,
Lasha Tilsen

Lasha Tilsen
3 Kennard ct.
St. Paul, MN 55106

The Healing Rosary

When we were in Mexico, I had with me a very special rosary that was hand crafted in Ireland. It was a gift from Phyllis Hooper, a dear friend who had given it to me when Kelly initially had surgery for his brain tumor. The rosary had been given to her years prior from a kind old Irish woman named Bridget. When Phyllis had been ill, the woman had given it to her and told her to pass in on to someone in need some day, that Phyllis would know when it was the right time. For me it was the right time. My son had been given a death sentence; I needed something to hold on too. That something, literally, was this simple wooden rosary.

The rosary is made of wooden beads with hand-carved shamrocks on each bead and finished with a simple silver crucifix . It came in a little pouch, and I always kept it in my pocket wherever I went, praying for an intercession, praying for a miracle. When we were in Mexico and attended the healing services in Maniadera, I had it with me. During the service this old woman who was apparently channeling the persona of Jesus had asked us all to come up individually and be blessed. I thought to myself that there are not that many opportunities to speak to Jesus in the first person, so I felt compelled to reach in my pocket and bring out the rosary to be blessed.

I walked up to the old woman and placed the rosary into her gnarled but gentle ancient hands. Raising the beads above her head in adulation, she blessed the beads, kissed the crucifix, patted it on the forehead of her bowed head and returned it to my hands. She then placed her hands firmly but lovingly on my head and told me that my faith was as big as a mountain and I was to become an apostle of God who would spread the word of what faith in God can do.

As you know, Kelly received a miracle it that little chapel in Mexico; his tumor disappeared. Six months later the cancer returned, claiming his young life. After Kelly died, my faith was tested as I fell into the valley of despair that I wallowed in for a seemingly endless span of years. I forgot about my apostolic duties, forgot about the rosary, forgot most things. As life moved forward, my healing progressed incrementally, and I merged back into the mainstream of life once again.

All those years the rosary silently collected dust, long since forgotten in the aftermath of broken dreams and raw survival. In the summer of 1999, as the world prepared to launch into the new millennium, a friend of mine was diagnosed with leukemia and needed a bone marrow transplant to save his life. He was unable to find a genetic match in the bone marrow data base but was fortunate to match genetically with the blood from the umbilical cord of healthy born baby in Italy. The transplant was completed, but his faith as well as his body were severely tested. He was looking for a miracle. It was then I remembered about the rosary collecting dust in my wife's jewelry box.

Both of us being Catholic, Barb and I were married and our children baptized in the Catholic Church. As a youngster I was made to follow church doctrine without question and found that, as an adult, I rarely recited the rosary. I always felt reciting the rosary was some sort of punishment or penance for sins I had committed—until that day in Mexico when I discovered its use in healing meditation.

When my friend David was having a very rough time following his transplant and things were touch and go, David started to attend Catholic Church again more regularly. It was then I had the supernal epiphany about the rosary and the possibility that it could help to heal David. I dusted it off and gave it to David almost as if instructed to do so. David has now recovered fully and is doing remarkably well. Ten years later he is still healthy and cancer free.

David was doing so well, less than a year later I asked him for the rosary back to give to another friend who was diagnosed with a difficult-to-treat form of cancer. David reluctantly released it to me like

Bilbo Baggins from the story of the *Hobbit* by J. R. R. Tolkien, who'd had to pass the ring of power to his nephew, Frodo. The rosary, like Bilbo's ring, was David's "precious," but he had to release its legacy.

I then traveled to Eau Claire, Wisconsin, to give the rosary to Troy, a friend in need. Troy is not Catholic, but he gratefully accepted the rosary—conventional medicine could not stop the progression of his disease, and he was seeking a miracle. With rosary in hand, Troy went out west for alternative treatments. The day of one of his treatments happened to be the vernal (spring) equinox, on or around March 20th of that year (2000). Prior to Troy's departure, we had networked to reach people from all over to stop what they were doing for a full minute at the exact time of the vernal equinox, the midway point of the one day when there are exactly twelve hours of light and twelve hours of darkness on the planet. Troy said he felt an amazing surge of energy at that moment and felt at complete peace and knew he would be healed. He went into remission following the treatments and is healthy today.

When we found out about Troy's remission, I soon traveled to Eau Claire again to retrieve the rosary for yet another person in need. Working in maintenance at the Catholic school, I had built a wheelchair ramp for this woman named Pam who was a mom of some kids in the school. With the ramp she could attend the weekly school Mass. She had been diagnosed with ALS (amyotrophic lateral sclerosis, also known as Lou Gehrig's disease), and I was compelled to approach her and give her the rosary. That was midwinter, 2001.

Pam loved the rosary and used it every day (you can tell by the wear marks on the rosary's wooden beads), and she said it helped her everyday through a long and difficult transition. I then had the awful task of asking her for the rosary back for my cousin's seventeen-year-old daughter, Kelsey, who had been in an accident January of 2003. Pam reassured me it was meant to move on; she had possession of it much longer than she ever thought possible. Pam then handed the rosary back to me and whispered, "Thank you so much. It has truly blessed my life." Months later she died but was at peace.

In the auto accident, Kelsey's car was totaled, her dog was killed, and she was left in an unresponsive coma. After receiving the rosary from Pam, I brought it to Kelsey, uncurled her white contracted fingers and placed the rosary in her palm. Like petals closing slowly at sunlight's waning, she grasped the rosary tightly. I told her it was a powerful instrument of God and would help her come back to this world and that Kelly, my son, would be there to help her through it. I kissed her on the forehead and left. As her Mom and I walked away, her hand shot up momentarily. The rosary beads swung from her clenched hand, which then fell motionless again to her lap. Her Mom said, "Oh my God, she just waved good bye to you." Of course the attending nurse assured us it was just a reflex. We knew better.

A year before, in January of 2002, a parent at the school named Gary who was a Minnesota state patrol officer was diagnosed and being treated for a rare form of cancer that was not responding well to treatment. He needed a stem cell transplant. Although a transplant did not offer a high chance of his survival, it was his only hope. He had four kids in my school, and I was praying I could give him the rosary some day when Kelsey no longer needed it.

Finally a miracle! The day before Easter, 2003, my cousin called and said Kelsey had awakened from her coma and that she was excited to see me and give the rosary back. I traveled to St. Cloud on Easter morning where I met with Kelsey. She smiled and hugged me, struggling to say thank you, she handed me back the rosary. Praise God for another miracle; it was a powerful moment I will not ever forget.

The next day I gave the rosary to Gary in its little wooden box that also held several other mementos of Kelly's and notes from previous rosary holders. His transplant was successful, and his recovery surpassed all odds. In early May of 2005, he stopped by the school, and this very large man embraced me with a huge hug and returned the rosary, saying he no longer needed it and felt strongly someone else might.

From Gary in reference to the rosary:
Mitch,

As I was reading your email, I was reminded of your son's belongings placed next to me on the hospital bed, all those many days. I would bring the container and open it up and place the rosary and contents on the stainless steel rolling desk, which was adjacent to my bed.

You may recall my story, where early on during my initial bout with cancer (January '02), I began to wrap a rosary around my wrist—the rosary would be placed around the IV tubes to the point where the medicine/ chemo would have to travel 'through' the rosary in order to enter my body. I always felt it was God's love which would allow the drugs to work their magic. The rosary provided the graces to rid my body of evil—cancer. In reality, the rosary was always there—but it was my devotion to Jesus, identified by the rosary to any who looked on, that was the real impetus behind my healing.

To this day, every evening before I go to bed, I continue to wrap a rosary around my right wrist—even when I'm away on vacation, I bring a rosary with me.

Let me know how I can help Mitch,

—Gary

A few days before Gary returned the rosary unexpectedly, we had found out a high school friend or ours, Debby, was diagnosed with pancreatic cancer, and we soon passed the rosary on to her. She was not given much time or any hope of survival. Debby was grateful for the extra time she had been given and so very grateful for the rosary that she felt may help to make that time possible. Debby died on January 2, 2005, some twenty months following diagnosis. She lived way beyond any realistic expectations for that disease. A month later the rosary was returned by Patti, Debby's sister. With it was this note:

Mitch and Barb,

Greetings! I am returning the beautiful story and rosary to you, in hopes that it can be passed along to another special person who could use a little help from above. Debby had it close to her the entire time. Thanks so much sharing it with her. Patti.

The next day I bumped into a mom named Lisa whose daughter had gone to the school where I work. I met her going into the chapel to pray. She was pregnant. I congratulated her, but she looked so sad. Lisa is the mom of Amanda, a dear little student friend of mine who had attended my school a few years back. She and Amanda were praying for Lisa's yet-to-be-born son, "Jeremiah Trinity," to heal his condition of hydrocephalus that had just been diagnosed along with kidney problems. There was much concern. Doctors were on high alert to be ready to assist with possible complications that could arise at birth; the prognosis was not good. I had found the next person who needed the rosary.

A month later Lisa told me that, based on the last ultrasound, it seemed the hydrocephalus had resolved itself. She told me that she had received her miracle. In prayer she was told someone else needed the rosary more now, so she wanted to give it back. I did not know yet to whom it was going next, but I said I would take back the rosary when she had time to drop it off.

A few days later I received two emails about a young boy in Hudson, Wisconsin, who had been diagnosed with a brain tumor. They were seeking my advice. One email had been written by an aunt of the boy and originally sent to the radio station where I had recently spoken. Barb of KDWA then forwarded me the message from this boy's aunt. The other email was forwarded to me from a friend who runs an Internet website in Atlanta with a message from another of Grant's aunts who was trying to reach me. I emailed Lisa about receiving the emails and asked about getting the rosary back.

Over the weekend we received the rosary from Lisa, and we brought it over to Grant, the nine-year-old boy with pontine glioma, a very deadly tumor. We sat with his mother, father, brothers, aunt, and grandma, and explained the story. Then we presented the rosary to Grant. That was Monday, March 20, 2007, and it was the vernal equinox. At precisely 12:26 p.m. Central time, the exact moment of the equinox, family, friends, and supporters of Grant from all over said a silent prayer for Grant's healing. At the same time in Hastings, Minnesota, the radio station KDWA also announced a moment of silent pray for Grant.

Grant rallied and was soon back in school, and with some limitations was doing very well. He loved having the rosary and kept it by his side.

On October 23, 2007, Grant succumbed to the disease and died. His parents still clung to the rosary in their devastating grief; it had been a daily part of their lives for almost two years. When they had the strength, they brought it over to our home. They did not have words adequate enough to express how much the rosary meant to them; the wooden beads had been further worn down from constant prayer. In the wooden box the rosary traveled in they placed a small bottle of Lourde's water also known for its curative powers. They also left in the box Grant's guardian angel pin and his favorite holy cards—Saint Frances, Saint Therese, Saint Peregrine, and his most favorite, Saint Michael.

On February 6, 2008, the rosary was blessed by the Arch Bishop of the Saint Paul Dioceses of Roman Catholic Churches, and only days later I received news of a young woman, a dear family friend, who had been diagnosed with third-stage multiple myeloma, a cancer of the blood. She was in the prime of her life with a husband and two little girls. She asked God for a miracle, so I gave her the rosary, all its energy, all its love and all its tears. Every hand that has held it dear has contributed a part to its living legacy, its healing, its testimony to faith, and the power of prayer that is within our reach. This young woman will hand me back this rosary sometime in the future, thanking God and passing it on.

I believe this rosary is very special and is one of a kind. I believe also that each person to have held this rosary and been healed of a challenging health condition has left their imprint on it in a very real way. Just as an Internet website can leave a cookie behind on your computer for a quicker connection to the site, so I believe a spiritual cookie is left upon the hard drive of the rosary. Each cookie is a powerful direct connect to God, others prayers, and hotline for healing. Just holding the rosary is an honor, but like a computer you need a password to connect. That password is prayer.

God's healing energy is always there for us. It's our faith that opens the channels of divine love and allows healing energy from every prayer that is said to travel down a direct line of love, and thus the healing begins. A healing is not always a cure, but it can bring comfort…if you believe.

The Circle of Life

Late in March of 2009, I received a call from an old classmate from high school, someone I had not talked to in over thirty years. She had lost a son to death some eight years earlier and had written a book, and she wanted to get it published. She just *happened* to contact my publisher at Beaver's Pond Press, not far from my home in Minnesota. My dear friend and mentor Milt Adams, the founder of Beaver's Pond, accepted her manuscript, which is now a Beaver's Pond new release (summer 2010). At that time Milt, had given her my contact information, and she called. We discussed publishing rhetoric for quite awhile, and of course our mutual losses. Following the loss of her son, she became more aware of her psychic abilities and pursued a career as a professional psychic, which is much of what her book is about.

During the latter part of our conversation, she commented that my son Kelly was "coming through." She said Kelly wanted to tell me that I was going to be a grandfather again soon and that he was coming back to our family. I was somewhat taken aback, to say the least, but excited about the possibility of being a grandfather again, to say nothing about the fact that this child could somehow be a reincarnation of my son Kelly. Wow! That was a lot to grasp.

Both my wife and my daughter Meagan thought it was just crazy talk; this stuff just does not happen. Meg told me, "Dad I am on the pill. My husband is losing his job. We may have to foreclose on our house. We have a three-year-old to care for. It is not in the cards for a pregnancy for us. She is mistaken."

Three weeks later Meg, called me and relayed that she'd had several dreams of being pregnant. So she'd done a home pregnancy test, and it was positive! She made an appointment with the doctor, which confirmed her home test; she was indeed pregnant with a speculated due date of November 16th, 2009—Kelly's birthday.

We waited anxiously for November 16th to arrive, but it came and went without even a contraction. By the end of November it was becoming apparent the baby was way overdue; it was possible they would have to induce. Then, in the wee hours of December 1st, our second granddaughter, Olivia Kelly, was born. Not on Kelly's birthday, as we had thought, but on the same day twenty-three years earlier that Kelly had died.

Can it be true that Kelly reincarnated twenty-three years to the day from his death? Did he come back as my granddaughter as foretold by a psychic? Is he back in spirit as my grandchildren's guardian angel? Did he arrange this gift so that he could move on to other realms only dreamed of? I truly have no idea. Facts are facts, which speak for themselves. Can anything really be proven or, for that matter, even need to be proven? What is soul anyway? Can it come back? Does it reside in heaven forever, or is it a multi-dimensional energy weaving itself through the ages ad infinitum?

Everything we know about the universe is more or less speculation of the arrogant human brain. The more we know, the more we know we don't know. We are all blind men describing the real elephant in the room with information derived from our other senses and the culmination of total input our brain has received. All I know is that I smiled on a day that had normally been reserved for tears.

The circle of life is just that
There is no death, a circle has no end
There is no end or stopping point
Only transitions and new-found friends

There is a light at the end of every tunnel
It's the same light at either end
Life is a tunnel and a forever circle
Where every beginning…was once an end

"Tears are shed when we are born and they usher us out when we die;

the meaning in life is a dance in between."

—MC

The 20 Faces of Grief©

Throughout the pages of this book, you will find portraits of grief used as illustrations for quotes and poems. This series of pencil portraits were created over a period of several years. Each one is a composite from photos, people, and feelings that I have observed in walking the walk with the bereaved. I tried to create a likeness of many of the emotions that I believe are integral to the journey in surviving the loss of a loved one.

Although there may be more emotions not characterized here, I believe these are fundamental, archetypal images, and each one stands out on its own. Many of these emotional components can be experienced alone or in concert with each other, and some may never be experienced at all—every journey is so unique.

In the long-term journey of surviving the loss of a loved one, the accepted five stages of grief just do not adequately apply. Denial, anger, bargaining, depression, and acceptance were derived from research with the dying, not the bereaved, and have been misapplied ever since. Although these stages may be relevant to those hearing the news of their own diagnosis of terminal illness or that of a close loved one, they do not adequately represent the long-term grief journey.

A stage implies a linear progression of events. Grief is a journey; it is not an illness or a stage one goes through. It begins with shock and then becomes a multifaceted journey to acceptance. There are no stages, only emotional components that may come and go and fluctuate in intensity the rest of our life.

The emotion that I applied to each portrait when I created it is listed here with their corresponding page numbers for matching illustrations throughout the book. One can use the illustrations from the book with the instructions that follow or order a small group kit which contains a set of 8"× 5"cards and a DVD slide show. A perfect tool for group or chapter meetings, it can be used to conduct a small workshop. For more information go to: www.heartlightstudios.net

How to Use the 20 Faces of Grief©

These faces were created for use in small group settings to give insight into and stimulate the bereavement process.

While these images may capture the major emotions associated with loss, they are not all inclusive, nor will you necessarily experience all of them on your personal journey.

Please study each drawing individually. Then, in your own words, describe the emotion you think it represents and/or what emotions are triggered when viewing the image. As the artist I have a personal concept of what each image represents to me, but they can be different for each person. Go by your first impulse. Only the first and last images are intentionally placed in that position; the rest are placed in completely random order, with no intentional sequencing of events.

Group leader: Please take care not to reveal the verbiage on the back of each card or explain their meaning ahead of time. You can, however, read the names of the twenty emotions I have listed to give participants a general idea on how to respond. The intent is to provoke self-intro-spection and identification of their personal journey; there is no right or wrong answer. Please provide pen and paper for participants to record their responses and reactions to the images as they are presented.

It is recommended to show each card for a few minutes and then have participants record their reaction. Go on to the next card, one at a time, until all twenty cards have been shown. Upon request show individual cards by number if someone needs to view them again, or you might briefly run through the entire deck once more. To conclude show each card as they were presented the first time and ask for input from participants from their recorded notes. Then read verbiage on the back of card and share viewpoints.

▶ **#1 Shock (page 91)**

Shock is a two-fold emotion.

First it can be that scream of terror that vibrates from your bones when you know or hear that your loved one has died. *It rocks your world!* You scream "NO!" to anyone and to everyone—"No this cannot be happening!"

Second, shock is the ongoing numbness that gives us the ability to even function. Shock is a fundamental survival tool of the human psyche that will last as long as it is needed to get done what is necessary for one's survival.

Although most of the bereaved go through shock when they face the reality that their loved has died, some facing a loss to long-term ill-ness will not. Survivors of loss to a long-term illness may, at first, feel a sense of relief followed by guilt for feeling that relief, but they not experience shock per se. They may feel the numbness component of shock that their loved one really has died but not the surreal surprise that accompanies sudden death.

▶ **#2 Loneliness (page 86)**

Loneliness is that profound sense of "missing them," that deep-seated feeling of wanting them back at our side, to hear them, see them, and to touch them.

Loneliness is where your heart and soul is surrounded with continual thoughts and memories of who your loved one was in your life.

Loneliness can be felt physically, where your body actually aches for their presence and you wish you could turn back the clock.

▶ **#3 Fear (page 15)**

Fear is that emotion that resonates from the core of our being, that natural survival tool that can illicit the flight or fight response. We either run from our fear or fight it; it is a primal instinct.

We have fear of forgetting, fear of an uncertain future, fear for the lives of our other loved ones, fear of losing our own sanity, fear of more pain, fear of not being in control.

▶ **#4 Anguish (page 133)**

Anguish is that emotion of extreme agony and pain that one feels in accepting the reality of the loss or news of the loss.

Anguish can produce a gut-wrenching paroxysm that cripples our resolve and wracks our bodies with the very real physical pain of loss.

Anguish is our heart and soul moaning.

Anguish is the first step toward acceptance that the loss is real.

▶ **#5 Hope (page 147)**

We as humans have the unique capacity among living life forms to cultivate hope. We can project into the future a longed for outcome.

Hope can be rather elusive early on in the grief journey and not even entertained or longed for in many cases.

But hope is natural; it is in our psyches and will try to sneak its way into our consciousness despite our attempts to keep it at bay.

Hope is looking for and seeing a light at the end of the tunnel.

Without hope there is only despair.

▶ **#6 Despair (page 41)**

Despair is that emotion that leaves you feeling helpless, hapless, hopeless, tired, sad, confused, fearful, and tearful.

It's hard to think, hard to function, hard to emote, hard to vent or cry our emotions; we are striving hard to even breathe. We feel paralyzed and stuck with no apparent way out.

The pain seems unending, our future bleak and unimaginable.

▶ **#7 Faith (page 106)**

Faith is having a belief in a higher power or in oneself to be able to overcome all odds.

To have faith is to live with confidence that recovery is possible and that finding peace and acceptance will one day be attainable.

Faith is maintaining a belief that there is life after death on both sides of the equation.

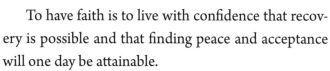

Faith gives us strength to take those first steps.

Faith is believing that, when we come to the edge of the unknown, in our next step we will find firm footing or be given wings with which to fly.

▶ #8 Depression (page 52)

Depression is that emotional state that can range from a sudden, momentary feeling of deep sadness to a clinical condition requiring medical attention.

Depression is not a stage but natural survival tool.

Depression is a state of profound sadness coupled with feelings of dejection and abandonment accompanied by a sharp decrease in mental acuity.

Depression is a survival tool to shut down the system, a "ctrl/alt/delete" for our souls, to sort things out at a deeper level and reboot our spirit to survive another tomorrow.

Depression can be a serious condition, especially with concurrent mental health issues. If depression lasts for an extended period of time and/or is accompanied by thoughts of suicide, medical attentions should be sought.

▶ #9 Confusion (page 154)

Confusion is a state of mental uncertainty, where perceptions are unclear and facts are mixed up. Focusing is difficult, and short-term memory loss profound.

This emotion is more prevalent in the early months following a loss but may linger for many years. Decisions are difficult to reach, and making plans becomes a formidable task.

Important decisions should not be made without counsel.

Buying Post-it notes, creating a journal, and making lists are encouraged to survive the pangs of confusion.

▶ #10 Anxiety (page 99)

Anxiety is a painful uneasiness of mind marked by an abnormal apprehension of anticipated problems, pressing issues, and expected pain.

In anxiety there appears to be no light at the end of the tunnel, and the journey seems an unending pervasive uphill climb.

Anxiety creates restlessness, indecisiveness, insomnia, and physically raises blood pressure and heart rate.

In anxiety tensions run high, and tempers often run short.

▶ #11 Denial (page 119)

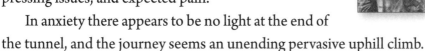

Denial is not always a bad thing; it gets us through to the next day and keeps us functioning.

Denial eclipses most other emotions and is meant as a survival tool, not a continuous-use tool.

We use denial as needed, moving in baby steps—but we eventually have to walk full stride or suffer in silence forever.

In the beginning, denial gets us through.

Denial in the long term is not healthy.

When we deny our feelings, when we hide our tears or over medicate our pain, then denial becomes an obstacle to recovery.

Denial is when we deny our laughter, our joy, and our destiny.

▶ #12 Self-isolation (page 81)

We experience self-isolation when we become reclusive and afraid of interacting with others; we avoid contact with people at large.

We do not want others' pity, or hear their bumbling attempts at compassion with trite, overused clichés that stab at our hearts.

We are feeling fragile and do not want to break down in public.

We have no want for joy or companionship; we want to wallow in our sorrow.

We have no time for the mundane nor any patience with others and their trivial priorities.

We do not want to hear about the joys and accomplishments of others.

We want to be alone and left alone.

Left in this emotion too long, one can become agoraphobic, which literally means the "abnormal fear of being in a helpless, embarrassing, or inescapable situation characterized by avoidance of open or public places."

▶ #13 Guilt (page 26)

Guilt is a very pervasive emotion on the grief journey, whether it's real, perceived, or imagined.

This is where the shoulda, woulda, couldas bombard your being.

One can struggle with self blame, ignorance, misgivings, past mistakes, poor choices, lack of perception, lack of foresight, and countless other ways to beat oneself up in an apparent failure to prevent the loss.

We can feel guilt on many levels, from guilt for actually causing the death to guilt for feeling relief.

We can feel guilt for laughing, eating, playing, feeling good again, or even loving again.

▶ **#14 Melancholia (page 66)**

Melancholia is a state of "sweet sorrow," an active, self-willed sadness or moroseness.

We have choices. We can wallow in our sorrow and immerse ourselves in our grief, or we can try to deny it. It is our grief, and we need to process it and move through it. Melancholy is cathartic; it feels good to surround ourselves with thoughts of our loved ones, the good memories and the bad.

Melancholia and denial are not shipmates.

Melancholia is active grieving, picking at the scab of our wound, feeling the pain and the pleasure. While experiencing the pain of our loss, we simultaneously feel the pleasure by remembering wonderful moments with our beloved.

Sometimes we can express our melancholy in an almost enthusiastic way to a point of lugubriousness that may be unsettling to those non-grievers around us. We can become over-the-top in our lamentations and lose touch with reality.

Melancholia is integral to healing and should be used as needed or as compelled for the short term, but it should not become a continual state of existence.

▶ **#15 Rage (page 74)**

Rage is a deep-seated reactionary anger from within that erupts quickly with violent and explosive overtones.

Although many in grief experience anger, not everyone experiences rage.

In cases of murder, reckless behavior, or medical mistakes, rage is a very real component of the bereavement process.

Rage is the scream of injustice, incomprehensibility, and extreme anger stemming from our lack of control over the situation or our inability to protect our loved one.

Although rage is a natural reaction and needs to be expressed, its actions can be deleterious to oneself and to others if not controlled.

▶ #16 Sadness (page 95)

Sadness is the outward expression of lamentations. Sadness is most often accompanied by tears, unbridled crying, weeping, whimpering, and moaning.

Sadness is a pervasive element of the grief journey that can erupt at any moment. Although not always at the forefront of our journey through grief, it is a continual and integral part of mourning the loss of a loved one.

Sadness comes and goes and usually brings tears and is often accompanied by her sister emotions, despair and loneliness.

Sadness is letting it out, expressing it, and sharing your pain.

▶ #17 Frustration (page 70)

Frustration is a common element in the grieving process; it happens when you realize you cannot fix things and make everything better.

Frustration results from not recognizing or acknowledging the new "normal" that is developing in your life. Life will never be the same, but you desperately want everything to be as it was.

Frustration is not getting done what you used to.

Frustration is not being able to feel better.

Frustration is having no apparent choices.

Frustration is not seeing our loved one.

Frustration is living when you want to die.

Having to move forward is frustrating.

Not understanding any of this is frustrating.

▶ #18 Anger (page 80)

Anger is a natural reaction to loss of any kind, especially when things happen beyond our control, and death is always, ultimately, beyond our control.

Anger produces endorphins and adrenaline that provide the needed energy for survival and pain reduction.

Anger releases stress and tension.

Anger can be a motivator for action.

Anger directed *appropriately* can be a positive agent for change.

Anger *unexpressed* can be deleterious to oneself.

Anger can be easily misdirected; discretionary use is advised.

▶ #19 Apathy (page 112)

Apathy can be a very prevalent emotion in the early years of loss. It is when a total lack of emotion seems to surround your being.

You become indifferent to world issues, other people's problems, or even struggles of your own.

You couldn't give a rip about the joys or celebrations of others. Life has lost all its zest, and living on or moving forward seems a meaningless option.

Apathy is when life loses all its color; everything seems gray.

Apathy knows no smile, frown, or scream.

In apathy you just don't care.

Apathy can often be accompanied by his brother depression.

▶ **#20 Peace (page 138)**

Peace is always attainable but not always reached on the grief journey or even in life itself. Peace is illusive for many years following the loss of a love one, and in some cases it can elude us for a lifetime.

Peace is finding ultimate acceptance with the *physical* loss of a loved one in your life.

Peace is letting go of what can never be and accepting what is.

Peace is getting better, not bitter.

Peace is not letting go of our loved one but holding on to their memory and their spirit.

Peace is finding joy again.

Peace is falling in love again.

Peace is not getting over your loss but living with it.

Peace is not moving on; it's moving forward.

Peace is embracing your destiny.

Peace is turning loss into legacy.

Peace can bring serenity.

The portraits below are pencil drawings that I have created for families who have lost a child in their lives.

Gone from our arms but not our hearts.

For more information on commissioned portraits,
go to: www.heartlightstudios.net

Postscript from the First Edition

December 1, 2001

On December 1, 1987, my world was shattered by the death of my son. I had lost my father at age fifteen; being the youngest of seven children, I knew him as a father, but never as a friend. My son then died at age nine, and I again lost a longed-for future friend. I will never know Kelly as an *adult* friend, although, through the process of Kelly's illness and with the knowledge of his impending death, we did in a way become friends, for we were buddies. Despite all the pain and horror in the last two years of his life, we truly lived life to the fullest; we shared more life in a short time than many families would in a lifetime. I recognize that now, and it gives me some solace from the painful memories.

Today is December 1, 2001, fourteen years to the day, following Kelly's death. The final touches on the manuscript are finished and will go to the publisher on Tuesday. Toward the end of the book you may have read the poem, "Where Do We Go from Here?" In that sonnet, I ask the question, "Where has all the magic gone that once had filled my life?" So many miraculous experiences surrounded us at the time that we tended to take them for granted. Life moves on regardless of situation, and so do we.

In the poem, I lament not having experienced any more mystical communications or experiences from Kelly. Had Kelly moved on or had I? I was content with the message of the cornstalks and truly expected nothing more. That's part of the letting go or moving on that we hear about so often. It is not letting go of our child, but letting go of the old expectations for *our* perceived future.

Finishing the book that I had promised Kelly I would write was a huge step in *not* letting go. People have said to me, "This book must finally be bringing you some closure." I have retorted to them, "No, closure is a myth perpetuated by others uncomfortable with our grief." There is no closure when a child dies; on the contrary it's a world of new beginnings. The only closure that we seek is that with our stolen dreams; when we let go of the should-have-beens that will never be, we make room to embrace the could-bes that are yet possible.

When Kelly was first diagnosed, a neighbor and good friend of ours in Bayport gave Kelly a beautiful blue-eyed white Siamese cat that she had picked up at the shelter. Kelly named him Ernie, and they became fast friends and inseparable. When they were sitting together in the right light, their intense blue eyes of the same shade glowed brightly. It was very striking. After Kelly's death, Ernie became a loner and a recluse, hiding in the shadows and very rarely interacting with anyone.

A few months ago, Ernie, now almost nineteen years old, became sick and we had to put him down. When my wife returned home from the vet with Ernie in a box, I dug a hole in our back pasture in preparation for burial. Ernie, still warm, was lying as if just asleep in a box in our basement when Kathy, an old friend, stopped by unannounced. She was that good friend from the Bayport days who had given Ernie to Kelly some fourteen years earlier. She was surprised and saddened by the death of Ernie. She said, "Guys, I had no idea about Ernie, but look what I have in the truck." We went to her vehicle and we found, sitting on the front seat, a beautiful five-week old Siberian Husky. The dog had the same white coloring of Ernie and, more strikingly, the same intense blue eyes. Kathy said, "Someone had dropped her off on a country road, and I was taking her to the shelter, but I thought you guys would have the room out here. And she is so beautiful." I took one look those dog's eyes and told our friend Kathy, "We'll take her!"

I am a real softy when it comes to animals and have always had a dog at the foot of our bed. Louise, as we call her now, regularly sleeps in our bed at night. Oddly, she always moves up right next to my head, by my pillow, in the same spot that Ernie had always slept. She is still a puppy, so at this time does not take up too much room. She is well behaved; I enjoy her presence and allow her to sleep there.

Last night I had a dream that I was in a bookstore and a woman was looking at my book and said, "My God, what an incredible story you two have to tell!" I then realized that my son Kelly, now my height, was standing right next to me, shoulder to shoulder. My left arm was crooked around his neck, our heads turned looking right into each other's eyes, and he smiled and said rather sheepishly, "I was pretty young. I don't remember that much of it anymore." I was so shocked at seeing him, I could say nothing, and with my arm still around his neck I pulled him closer. Looking into his eyes, I felt his energy and smelled his familiar scent. It was then that I woke up and found myself looking straight into the big blue eyes of my dog Louise. Her head was tightly crooked into my arm; her nose was on my chest. With her tail wagging wildly she smothered me with sloppy puppy kisses. No, the magic is never ever gone, and once again for Kelly and me, it was "hello and not goodbye."

—Mitch Carmody

About the Author

The author experienced a lot of death in his family at an early age and after he started his own family. During that time, he has studied much about the processes of death, dying, loss, and bereavement. In the process, he has found himself on a spiritual road of discovery that has continued to bless his life and ours.

Mitch is a trained hospice volunteer, as well as a trained massage therapist and AIDS Massage volunteer. He has facilitated many grief, cancer, massage, and stress relief groups and has taught classes at community education in these areas. Personally assisting people and their families struggling with terminal illness and grief is an important part of his ministry. He considers assisting to help plan and participate in funerals an honor and tries to help in making the experience a celebration of life.

He is a staunch supporter and volunteer with the American Red Cross and donates blood monthly. Helping others is paramount in his life, and he tries to help heal the human condition wherever he finds it.

The author is also a gifted photographer and an accomplished artist. He is responsible for the book's cover photograph of his son, Kelly, as well as many other award-winning photographs. He has completed hundreds of portraits of people, using a variety of mediums. More recently, Mitch has concentrated his artistic endeavors on his favorite medium, which is pencil and paper. Most of the illustrations used in this book are recent examples of the artist's work. The photo realism style you find in these portraits is evident in all of his art. He works out of his studio in Denmark Township, Minnesota, where limited-edition prints are available as well as custom portraits.

Mitch's wife, Barb, is an ICU (Intensive Care Unit) RN working at Lakeview Hospital in Stillwater, Minnesota. They were high school sweethearts and have been married since 1976. His daughter Meagan is now a mother of two beautiful girls, Kinsey Marie and Olivia Kelly. She works as nurse in Rochester, Minnesota. Mitch and Barb live on a small hobby farm in rural Denmark Township, just east of the Twin Cities on the Wisconsin–Minnesota border. The greatest love in their life is their granddaughters. Letting go of what should have been, but never letting go of their son—they have embraced life.

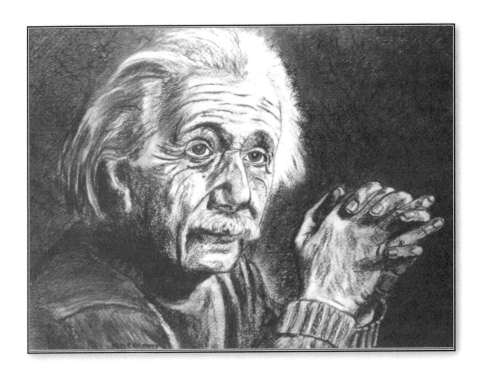

Man is here for the sake of other men—above all for those upon whose smile and well being our own happiness depends, and also for the countless unknown souls, with whose fate we are connected by a bond of sympathy.

—Albert Einstein

Message from the Author

I have recently begun work on my second book that will be titled: *Whispers of Love, the Language of Soul Speak.* This book will be a collection of letters from *you,* the reader. I am asking that you send in your stories of survival. If you have survived a devastating loss in your life and have found a meaningful existence once again, please send me your story. If you have survived a terminal illness or had a close brush with death, please send me your story. If you have received some form of communication from a lost loved one, please send me your story. If you had a prior-to-death experience, such as an omen or knowing or inkling of the tragedy, please send me your story. If you have had a near-death experience, please send me your story. If you have a story of someone who has been a "parachute" in your life and provided a pathway for your healing, please send me your story. I know there many more life-changing stories of survival that need to be shared.

Please send all correspondence to:

Heart Light Studios Inc.
14765 70th St. South
Hastings, Minnesota 55033

Websites: www.heartlightstudios.net
www.proactivegrieving.com

Email: heartlightstudio@aol.com